Wessex Stitchery

By Gay Eaton

"A little sampler for the month of May work'd while skies were warm and flowers were gay And all good British people humbly pray'd that Peace with Victory be not delay'd"

Bath Abbey

B. Butler

GPL GEORGESON PUBLISHING LIMITED

WESSEX STITCHERY

Published by Georgeson Publishing Limited

P.O. Box 100-667, North Shore Mail Centre, New Zealand 1330.

Ph: 649 410 2079, Fax: 649 410 2069

Email: gpl@georgeson.co.nz, Web Site: www.georgeson.co.nz

We have made every effort to ensure that these instructions are accurate and complete. We cannot, however, be responsible for human error, typographical mistakes, or variations in individual work.

ISBN No 0958210551

Editor: Prue Georgeson

Photography:

    Colour Plates: Maria Sainsbury

    Stitch patterns: Gay Eaton

    Melbourne Panel: Ian Cross

Illustrations and Layout: Andreena Buckton, Noodle Design Corp.

Printed: Hong Kong

Many people helped me in my research of Wessex Stitchery and Mrs Foster. I would particularly like to thank Jan Chester of Melbourne and her sister Josie Pedler of Bristol who undertook the initial valuable detective work and found Mrs Joan Ackland of Bath. I am very grateful to Joan Ackland for sharing her childhood memories of Margaret Foster and to Barbara Butler, also of Bath, for further details and the photographs she took of the places associated with Mrs Foster. I acknowledge the support that Sybil Goulden of Cheshire and Mary Guest, the President of the Mid-Wessex Branch of The Embroiderers' Guild of Bath gave me in my search for information. With the generous help and interest of these friends of embroidery we now know a little more about Mrs Margaret Foster and her Wessex Stitchery.

I am also indebted to Lynn Szygenda Deputy Director, Curator of the Embroiderers' Guild, Hampton Court Palace, London, for showing me a copy of the catalogue from the exhibition of Wessex Stitchery held at the Medici Galleries, London, March 1934 and the review from *The Times* London 1934. The essay written by Margaret Foster for the catalogue has given a very much fuller picture of Wessex Stitchery, its author and her philosophy, than had previously been available.

To be able to include a previously unknown piece of Margaret Foster's work is a very special privilege. I am most grateful to the owner of the Melbourne panel for allowing her original signed piece of Wessex Stitchery to be included. This most exciting discovery was the highlight of my research. Thank you to all involved.

The late Miss Helen M Moran was the most influential embroidery educator in New Zealand. She brought to Dunedin, in 1928, the latest teaching methods and techniques available in Britain at that time. Her influence and encouragement, given to the Southern Guilds in the early days of their establishment, is still much appreciated and acknowledged throughout New Zealand. We owe a debt of gratitude to pioneers like Miss Moran who worked to ensure that embroidery remains a living vital tradition.
I would also like to thank my many students and friends in both New Zealand and Victoria, Australia, who encouraged me by their enthusiasm for Wessex Stitchery to write this book. My husband Neil who supported me and gave me time and space to pursue the research and preparation required and Owen Baxter for being on hand when I needed help and advice with my Macintosh. I am also very grateful to the editor and publishers Prue and Tony Georgeson for their enthusiasm for this book.

Finally I would like to thank Mrs Margaret Foster for her inspiration. Her embroidery fascinated and inspired me. Researching this technique has been a tremendously enjoyable and satisfying process. Developing it as a workshop to offer in both New Zealand and Australia has been stimulating. None of this would have been possible without Mrs Margaret Foster of Bath.

ACKNOWLEDGEMENTS

CONTENTS

Wessex Stitchery is a rich blending, and layering of colour, stitch and text. It is a technique that can be used as a 'bridge' to safely carry those who would like to be more adventurous with their embroidery to a freer style of work which gives the opportunity to experiment with colour blending and designing with stitch. Wessex Stitchery is also a valuable method to record events, family history and favourite quotations.

Though Wessex Stitchery is a counted thread technique, it does not have the restrictions usually associated with this type of embroidery. It is an ideal technique if eyesight is a problem as it can be worked on an 18-20 count fabric. Because only a few materials are required, it is the perfect embroidery to pick up and work on while listening to music, visiting a friend or travelling.

For those who like to work freely, Wessex Stitchery has a lot to offer. It can be combined with other techniques to give added interest to your work. I plan to include Wessex Stitchery with my machine embroidery on a background that has been layered and built up with fabrics.

There are many other possibilities of combining Wessex Stitchery with other types of embroidery. Include it within a Drawn Thread or Blackwork Band Sampler, or use it as a border pattern for table linen, the richly textured patterns would also look well with canvas work.

However you choose to work Wessex Stitchery, I do trust that you shall gain as much enjoyment and pleasure from this satisfying technique as I have.

Gay Eaton, Dunedin, New Zealand 2000

HISTORY

Wessex Stitchery is a little known technique that features the use of simple stitches to create a wide range of Stitch Patterns. Very little has been published about Wessex Stitchery and even less seems to be known about its designer, Mrs Margaret M. Foster of Bath, who was a most remarkable woman.

Wessex Stitchery enjoyed support in the 1920's and 30's and this was recognised with an exhibition sometime during 1929 or 1930 at 20 Pultney Street, Bath, and a further exhibition held at the Medici Galleries during March 1934 in London. The work was reviewed in a number of embroidery publications as well as *The Times*. Since then minimal attention has been paid to this technique which was largely forgotten until recent Embroiderers' Guild Publications[1].

Little is known about Mrs Margaret Foster apart from her embroidery, not even the date of her birth, which we believe was 1843. We do know that she lived for more than 90 years in a lifetime spanning the reigns of Victoria, Edward VII and George V. This was a period of major social, political and economic change. Mrs Foster lived through numerous wars, the American Civil, the Crimean, Boer and World War I. The Arts and Crafts movement of the latter part of the 19th Century influenced all crafts and many social changes were brought about by improved communications and transport both locally and internationally. These included the telegraph and telephone systems, opening of London's first electric Underground, the arrival of motorised transport, the opening of the Panama Canal and the arrival of aeroplanes. These were times of change in the role and status of women also with the first woman joining the House of Commons and Women's franchise in England. At the same time huge advances were made in science. Perhaps as a reaction to this fast changing world needlework maintained a sense of serenity and peace because Mrs Foster suggests that

"Needlework ... denotes so much of patience, of delicate fingering, of quiet homeliness...". [2]

We do know that for a period of time Mrs Foster and her daughter Beryl lived in Bath. The city roll shows her address in 1929-30 as 51 Great Pultney Road. They both attended the Roman Catholic Convent Church of St John's and it is thought Beryl may have entered a convent. It is quite likely Mrs Foster lived in the area for many years as in the Forward to the catalogue of the Medici Gallery exhibition it states that "for some years Bath has been the casket which enshrines this genius of the needle".[3]

Of her early years nothing is known but Mrs Foster was still stitching in her nineties, at the time of her exhibition at the Medici Galleries. "When she reached (this age) it was thought that her eyes were failing her and an oculist examined her. He reported that there was nothing wrong with her eyes, but that she was using glasses suited to an

---

[1] *Making Samplers*, The Embroiderers' Guild, David & Charles, RD Press, London 1993, *The Embroidery Studio*, The Embroiderers' Guild, David & Charles, London, 1993.

[2] *Wessex Stitchery* 1934 Exhibition Catalogue, Introduction written by Mrs Foster.

[3] *Wessex Stitchery* 1934 Exhibition Catalogue, Forward written by Major Sir Neville Wilkinson K.C.V.O., A.R.E.

B. Butler

51 Great Pultney Road, Bath

old lady and not one as young in sight and mind as she was."[4]

Wessex Stitchery uses simple stitches to create diverse Stitch Patterns. A good knowledge of stitches is essential "as each stitch is to embroidery what each note is to music".[5] With the stitches as the embroiderers' tool an extremely varied range of stitch patterns was developed by Mrs Foster and she proudly stated in her introduction to the exhibition at the Medici Gallery in 1934 "that no two pieces (in an exhibition of 300 pieces) were alike". The exhibition was the culmination of approximately 30 years of work. It was described as "a wealth of colour, pattern and technique, each piece differed from the other".[6]

Colour is an important part of Wessex Stitchery and Mrs Foster "used the colours of her garden and surrounding countryside as inspiration".[7]

The actual technique was part of the British movement of the times away from stamped embroidery or 'fancy work'.[8] Wessex stitchery is a counted thread technique which Mrs Foster describes in her introduction "as a lost art." She points out that "The danger of following a drawn line, copied many times results in deviation that will spoil the beauty of proportion, perhaps the most essential beauty of any design, the one most easily lost. Wessex work follows the threads of its foundation with very little counting once the main grid has been established".

With mastery of the stitches used, it is possible for an unlimited number of stitch patterns to be created and for Mrs Foster, the stitch patterns almost developed of their own accord.

"Mrs Foster draws with her needle. A piece of hand-woven linen, linen thread, cotton or silk and the work is ready to begin. To quote her own words:- ' A Wessex needle.......asks for no suggestion for pattern or design on paper or material; it can even produce good effects without any previous planning of the worker's thought and brain, for it has stitches of its own by the use of which patterns will, as it were, evolve themselves......'," [9]

Mrs Foster described her work as a new form of stitching. She modestly did not "presume to call it embroidery but only stitching or stitchery - Wessex Stitchery". As most of the embroidery "has been designed and worked" in that province. Bath, in Somerset, is part of the old Country of the West Saxons. Only the southern boundary has remained constant throughout, being the south coast, the northern, western and eastern boundaries have fluctuated with no definitive landmark to determine the borders. Wessex was an advanced Anglo Saxon Kingdom, the realm of the forward thinking, gifted King Alfred The Great. It was in Bath that Edgar, King of Wessex was crowned King of England in 973. By 1154 the kingdom of Wessex was recorded as being Cornwall, Devon, Dorset, Somerset,

[4] *The Times* London, March 1934.

[5] *The Times* London, March 1934.

[6] *Embroidery*, June 1934, Volume 11, No.3.

[7] *Embroideress*, circa 1922-1939, Volume 7, pp 1197-1199.

[8] *Twentieth-Century Embroidery in Great Britain to 1939*, Howard, C., Batsford, 1981

[9] *Embroidery*, June 1934, Volume 11, No.3. Review signed S.N.E.

Wiltshire, Hampshire and Berkshire, some 4000 square miles of England.[10] Wessex enjoyed a proud history in the arts, including painting, music, embroidery and metalworking and where embroidery had been encouraged by as Mrs Foster states "Kings and men of sanctity and genius" including St Dunstan councilor to King Edmund the Magnificent and subsequently Abbot of Glastonbury, King Edward the Elder and others, therefore it was most appropriate to call this "new form of would be artistic sewing... Wessex Stitching."

Much of Mrs Foster's work included lettering. The quotations come from various sources including the Bible, old English rhymes, hymns, prayers, the Litany, historical notes, Shakespeare, poets, memorials and calendars of Saints. Some are surrounded by borders and motifs others are divided by bands of pattern.

It was the wording on her sampler worked in May 1918, that sparked my initial interest in this technique as a method of recording items of historical interest. This sampler can be seen, illustrated in colour in 'Making Samplers'.[11]

Mrs Foster recorded on her sampler the following:

> *"A little sampler for the*
>
> *month of May work'd*
>
> *while skies were warm and*
>
> *flowers were gay And all*
>
> *good British people humbly*
>
> *pray'd that Peace with*

Victory be not delay'd"

From this little sampler we know that while Britain was enjoying a warm late Spring, the gardens were putting on a colourful display, the allied soldiers were fighting an horrific war in the trenches of France and Belgium. There must have been a day of prayer for peace that would have echoed throughout the Commonwealth. Such contrasts within this little embroidery still speak to us today and remind us of the sacrifice made by so many. My Dad was one of those soldiers in the British Army fighting for his King and Country on the battle fields of Europe. That day of prayer for peace is possibly not recorded anywhere else?

Surviving work is to be found in the collection of The Embroiderers' Guild London, and in private collections (see Melbourne Panel page 80.)

Though little is now known of Mrs Foster, her work still speaks to us today, of a woman who held high values, a woman of strong faith, an independent thinker, someone who did not follow the fashion in the style of embroidery of the day, but chose to speak with her own voice. It is from her writing for the catalogue and her embroidery that we get a better glimpse into her life, philosophy and methods of working.

[10] *Wessex and the South 800 - 1500,* Hinton D.A., J.M.Dent & Co Ltd, London, 1977

[11] *Making Samplers,* The Embroiderers' Guild, David & Charles, RD Press, London 1993

THE MELBOURNE PANEL

(illustrated on page 80)

The Melbourne Panel is a very beautiful piece of Wessex Stitchery, worked by Mrs Foster when she was approximately 88 years of age. It measures 12.5 x 30 cm and is held in a private collection in Melbourne, Australia. The Catalogue of the March 1934 exhibition of Wessex Stitchery, Medici Society Limited, lists 140 exhibits, plus other small items. This small panel is possibly exhibit No. 70. It is described as "Worked on hand-woven cotton-cloth with cotton threads, with words from St Paul. (Lindisfarne pattern)" As can be seen the cloth has been cut to within two or three threads of the embroidery. Originally this piece may have been mounted and framed, because there is just a little glue still attached to one small part of the top edge. The Melbourne panel features three borders, and lettering that identifies it as an original piece. The main stitch pattern is Lindisfarne II plus two narrow borders. Within the narrow borders Mrs Foster embroidered Wessex Stitchery, Lindisfarne patterns. ...1932..m.m.f. At the bottom right hand side is "Whilst we have time, let us work good to all men. see Ep. of s.Paul to Galatians. ch v1. V10". The fabric thread count is 30 to the inch, the threads used are stranded cottons.

The Lindisfarne pattern is not dissimilar to that illustrated in *Embroidery* Volume 23 Number 1 Spring 1972. That pattern was stacked, not the half drop style seen on the Melbourne piece. The Melbourne Lindisfarne pattern includes an ingenious configuration of long tail fly stitch used to 'draw' the shape within a decorative border of straight stitches. The fly stitch filling can be used successfully without the border and would be suitable for bands or blocks of colour and pattern. The Lindisfarne pattern on the Melbourne piece has been named Lindisfarne II because it is a recent discovery. Included amongst the diagrams of Wessex Stitches *Embroidery* 1934 is another very different style of Lindisfarne pattern, it is listed as number 7 see page 39. Both these Lindisfarne patterns are shown graphed on pages 39-40. The narrower of the other two borders looks a little like Vandyke stitch, however study of the back of the panel showed that it was not that stitch and I have not been able to replicate it exactly. The closest I could come to it is the stitch pattern called Ritchie see page 49. It is a row of close herringbone as a base for broad chain stitch, the needle going into the fabric at the beginning and end of the chain stitch row only. The other narrow border is built up with wave, back and cross stitches and has been named Victoria, chart page 51. The lettering Mrs Foster used for the Melbourne panel is Alphabet I page 22. This alphabet is quite small and has a narrower script than is usual making it very suitable for small items. Where the Melbourne panel differs from those previously illustrated is the way that the colours have been used. At first glance it could seem as if an accident had occurred and something had been spilt over this piece. However on close scrutiny it readily shows a very skilled method of counter changing the dominant colours from the dark navy to the grey/blue and smaller quantity of grey/green. The grey/blue and grey/green are both the same colour value. The red and gold portions of the pattern remain constant, this keeps the basic shape intact, throughout the piece. This counterchange of colour also occurs on the narrower borders.

Mrs Foster made little effort to finish the threads off neatly, they can be seen on the back carried from one motif to the next, and left to hang loose when finished with. It is as if she enjoyed the stitching, but was under pressure to complete as many exhibits as possible (see page 80).

This wonderful piece of Margaret Foster's work, was brought into my Wessex Stitchery workshop in Melbourne. The owner gave the class the opportunity to see an original work and me the privilege of closely examining and gathering further information about this fascinating technique. The discovery of this piece of embroidery was the highlight of my research into this technique.

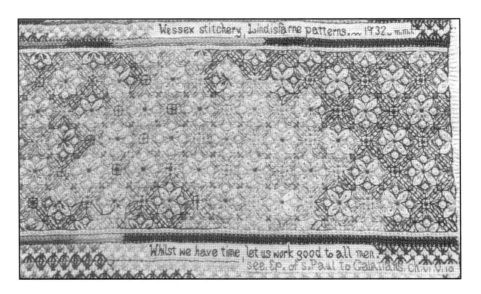

REQUIREMENTS

Fabrics

Wessex Stitchery is a counted thread technique. Mrs Foster describes it as "being simple enough, for it is guided only by the threads of the fabric, not a drawn line". Select even weave fabric, that is a fabric with the same number of threads to the warp as the weft. Choose a close weave that will support heavy stitching and allow threads to be carried across from motif to motif without showing through to the right side. The fabrics that I have enjoyed using are 32 count Belfast, 28 count Glenshee, 25 count Lugana and 35 count Edinburgh - these are given as a guide only. A good reason to choose the 28 and 32 count linens is because the stitch blocks can be as large as 24 x 24 threads so whilst you might be working on a fine linen the stitching is on a larger scale than needlepoint or cross stitch.

Wessex Stitchery may also be worked on an 18 - 20 count linen to create beautiful cushion covers and bags, but use tapestry wool or Perle Cotton No 5 for the embroidery. This count would be helpful for those who have difficulty seeing the finer linens and threads.

One of my teaching samplers is a 20 count linen and the stitch pattern sampler illustrated on the cover is worked on a cotton fabric with 28 threads to the inch. It was a fabric of unknown origin but because of its bulkier thread and close weave I have found it ideal for Wessex Stitchery. A variety of fabrics can be used for Wessex Stitchery, the important requirement is that they are even weave. Bearing this in mind choose a fabric that suits your eyesight and the project you have in mind and allow generously for the amount of fabric required.

Fabric: Evenweave linen to suit your project and eyesight!

HANDY HINT: To cut fabric straight, withdraw a thread.

Threads

Wessex Stitchery is a wonderful opportunity to delve into your thread collection as a wide selection of thread types can be included within any one piece of work. I have used DMC, Anchor, Semco plus threads from my grandmother's work basket in just one design. The sheen of stranded cottons and texture of Perles, which reflect the light, contrast well with the matt finish of Coton a broder and flower thread and combine most successfully within a pattern block to create a harmonious composition. Wessex Stitchery uses the variation of texture and colour to advantage. Many of the DMC and Anchor thread colours are available in various thread types and use the same colour coding making it simple to mix and match different weights and textures as required. This stitchery is also a good excuse to purchase an even better range of threads and colours to obtain just the right colour value, shade or texture for the project you have in mind!

Threads to use

- DMC and Anchor stranded cottons using as many threads as required.

- No 8 Perle Cotton, this gives texture and reflects the light, as well as contrasting with the finer stranded cottons. It works very well on the 28 count Glenshee and 32 Belfast.

- Coton-a-broder 16 and 25

- Select any of your favourite threads that give the colour and effect required, flower threads and silks would work well.

- lettering use one thread of stranded cotton,

- Three threads of stranded cotton are approximately equal to No 8 Perle cotton and can be substituted for the Perle in most instances. The choice of Perle 8 or two or three threads of stranded cotton depends upon the density of pattern wanted. If you require a very bold textural look, as in the Hussifs, choose the Perle 8, if you are wanting a softer more open appearance choose one or two threads of stranded cotton.

- Coton a broder 25 equates to two threads of stranded cotton and Coton a broder 16 equates to three threads of stranded cotton and No 8 Perle.

- For 18 - 20 count fabrics use tapestry wool (one strand of Appletons has been used on the cushion page 80) and No 5 Perle.

- A wide selection of thread types can be included within a piece of work

- Each design has the threads it has been stitched with listed.

- The threads used in the stitch pattern photographs are also given as a reference.

When stitching your own designs, the threads to use on any linen will depend on the effect you wish to create. Try working the stitch pattern you have chosen on the linen of your choice using different weights of thread and select the effect which pleases you. There are no absolutes - just new possibilities!

HANDY HINT: If the thread knots, try threading the needle from the opposite end. To loosen a knot, prise it apart with two needles.

Always select quality threads that are colour fast. It is disappointing to complete work, then find that colour has bled into the fabric or that the colours have faded.

Needles

A tapestry needle is used for all the stitching that is worked to the counted thread. The size will depend upon the thread being used, the fabric count and ease of threading. Needle sizes are given as a guide only, use the size that works for you! Do not persevere with a needle that is hard to thread! Try a No 24 for 25 - 29 count linen and a No 26 for 29 - 35 count linen.

Change to a crewel needle, that will pierce the weave of the fabric for the stitches that are not worked to a thread count, for example the fly, chain and straight stitches in Dunstan, Glastonbury, or the Wanaka Maze patterns. Again the size of needle used on the different linens will vary according to your personal preference, eyesight and threads used but I would suggest a size 8 crewel needle would work well with most linens, though a thicker needle would be advisable if you were using 20 count fabric and wool.

HANDY HINT: When buttonhole stitching around the edge of a small project use a larger needle (try a crewel needle No 5) at the corners - the larger needle makes space to carry the thread through the extra fabric.

If having difficulty threading needles, check that the eye has not dented, cut the end of the thread straight, apply a little lick, hold the thread firmly between your thumb and first finger so that it does not protrude and squeeze to flatten. Place the eye of the needle just where the thread is hidden, then roll the thumb and first finger back to reveal the thread and allow it to 'pop' into the needle.

Frame

For better stitch tension and to avoid puckering fabric, use a round frame. I find a small frame the best as my finger is able to guide the needle and thread movements under it. To improve the grip, the inner ring should be wrapped with either white or cream bias binding. The non-colour binding avoids the possibility of dye rubbing off, or bleeding onto your work. The other good reason to use a frame for embroidery is that it aids posture, allowing you to sit straight at your work.

HANDY HINT: If the linen you wish to use is too small to fit in your frame, extend it by machining calico or something similar along each side. Use a long stitch so it is easy to unpick.

While stitching, maintain good posture. Every so often get up, stretch, exercise fingers and hands to reduce tension and relax.

Scissors, Notebook & Pencil

For future reference it is good to keep notes of thread numbers and stitch patterns used.

Measure

A 15cm (6") ruler is very useful. I use it to measure the linens when tacking, especially for a 1 cm hem allowance. It fits within my little work bag or box and because it is rigid - I find it more useful than a tape measure.

Stiletto

A very useful tool to have in your work basket: for enlarging a space to carry a (finger) cord into a toggle, to lift and unpick tacking threads, to poke folded corners back in place when tacking and/or working edging stitches.

Magnifier

This may be required if working on dark coloured fabric especially when establishing the main patterns blocks.

BEFORE YOU BEGIN

or Starting, Finishing and other really useful techniques

Charts

- **On all the charts in this book each line represents one thread of fabric.**

- **Where notches are shown on charts these indicate the end of stitches.**

- **Colours mentioned in the instructions with the stitch patterns pages 34-64 relate to the charts not the photographs.**

The number of threads that each pattern is worked over can readily be changed allowing the designs to be enlarged or reduced in scale to suit your purpose or fabric count. More detailed information about this is given with the different stitch patterns.

VARIATIONS TO STITCH PATTERNS

Where variations of the stitch patterns have been used in different designs this is mentioned under stitch patterns and in the general text.

TO NEATEN RAW EDGES OF FABRICS:

Strengthen and secure the raw edges of even weave fabrics with sewing machine stitching. Use a matching fine to medium weight sewing thread top and bottom, the edging will be hidden in the hems.

- Select the serpentine stitch or a multi stitch zig zag, not the single stitch zig zag designed for buttonholes.

- Set the width to cover four to five threads of the cut fabric edge only and select a very short stitch length.

- Allow the machine to feed the fabric evenly, do not pull it through.

The machine stitches into the fabric weave and holds the warp and weft threads together in a very strong edge that can be left in place, and hidden in the turn-under for hems. The raw edges of linen samplers that I have used constantly in the classroom for twenty five years have been securely held in place by this method, without any further hemming.

TACKING: Select good quality, colour fast machine thread, in a colour that can be easily seen. If necessary colour code tacking.

- It is important to tack accurately over and under the number of threads the stitch pattern is divisible by, usually three or four threads.

- To mark the centre of a project tack the linen from top to bottom then tack from side to side.

- Start the second line of tacking at the centre - the stitches must not cross. Bring the needle out at the centre, leave a long thread trailing and tack to one side. Then rethread the needle and starting at the centre tack out to the other side.

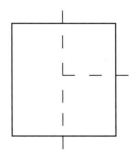

- Take tacking threads right to the edge of the fabric and leave ends trailing 2 cm (1") beyond fabric edge.

To begin stitching

Select the method that is suitable for the stitch pattern and threads,

1. Approximately 6 cm (2 1/2") from where you wish to begin stitching work one back stitch on the face of the work, this will avoid thread tangling (no need for waste knots), then bring your thread over to where you wish to begin stitching. Once there is enough stitching completed this thread can be finished off securely and neatly in the back of the work. This method is good for Perle, Coton a broder and multiple stranded cottons.

2. Double a long single thread of stranded cotton; thread the needle with the cut ends; bring the needle from the back over the fabric threads to make a stitch, then to the back again; hold in place by threading the needle through the end loop; the first stitch is made. I chose this method for the tray cloth to keep the back neater.

To start a new thread invisibly & finish an old one

- Secure a new length of thread into the back of the work when there is only 5 - 6 cm (2 - 3") of thread left in the needle and prior to neatening the nearly finished thread.

- Bring the new thread out in the exact same place as the nearly finished thread.

- Continue stitching the pattern with the new thread.

- Now neaten the finished thread under the stitching.

This method of bringing in a new thread, prior to finishing off the old one avoids 'loosing the place' and having gaps or breaks showing in your stitching. It is a useful technique for many types of embroidery.

Carrying threads & the back of your work

Wessex stitching is all about using and blending colour and pattern making, often working with two to six needles and different coloured threads at a time. It is not as tidy on the back as most other counted thread techniques because multiple threads need to be carried across from pattern block to pattern block and there are not the usual satin stitch blocks to slip threads under. Where possible carry the threads under the stitches already made taking care not to pull them too firmly. Working with the fabric held in a frame, should eliminate the risk and disappointment of puckered fabric when threads are pulled too tightly across patterns.

The reverse side of Mrs Foster's Melbourne piece illustrated on page 80 has an amazing entanglement of threads on the back. This clearly illustrates that she took little trouble to weave threads in behind the patterns and may have worked with more than one threaded needle at a time, as suggested in Colour Blending page 19, to achieve the effect she wanted.

Lining

It is important when using a woven fabric for lining, to fold the fabric along the straight grain of the material. Place this centre fold over the tacked centre line of the linen and pin or tack to hold in place. Time and care taken tacking saves time in the long run and gives a superior end result.

WESSEX STITCHERY

A unique feature of Wessex Stitchery is the many and varied stitch patterns that can be achieved with just a few simple, easily mastered stitches. Though others have extolled and illustrated this possibility, it was Mrs Margaret Foster of Bath who made pattern making with stitch, an art form.

It is the way the stitches are combined with each other and colour to create a wealth of intricate, decorative patterns that is exceptional. Wessex Stitchery is a technique that can be expanded with new stitch combinations tried and further patterns developed. Some stitches are worked in a way that will give a curved line to the pattern, a particular feature of Wessex Stitchery.

Wessex Stitchery 'sings out' to encourage embroiderers to have fun playing with colour and finding the many exciting combinations that can be achieved. It also 'sings out' to encourage you to experiment with combining colours that are not favourites, always a challenge! This is the reason you have been collecting such a wide range of embroidery threads 'that will come in useful one day'. What better excuse for an extensive thread collection than to experiment with Wessex Stitchery!

Wessex Stitch Patterns

Writing for the introduction to the exhibition at the Medici Gallery, London in 1934, Mrs Foster stated that there were nearly 500 stitch patterns all different from each other (within the 300 exhibits). Mrs Foster gave her stitch patterns names of local interest, unfortunately most of her patterns and their names are not now known. The 1932 Melbourne Panel (page 80) has three stitch patterns and the May 1918 sampler illustrated in 'Making Samplers' includes eight. Of those listed in *Embroidery* June 1934 and Spring 1972 only four of the stitch pattern names are given: 'Lindisfarne', 'Nigella', 'Margaret' and 'Steepholm'. A square of long tail chains listed as a favourite I have taken the liberty of naming Mrs Foster, in her honour.

Some of the stitch patterns from the Embroiderers' Guild publications are as illustrated, others such as Wanaka Maze, Margaret, Mrs Foster, Noughts and Crosses I have added embellishment to the original. Adding and developing the technique further, to reflect the message or purpose of a design, is an ongoing process.

The stitch patterns have been named for the magnificent cathedrals of Wessex and the places where I have taught this technique, in Dunedin, New Zealand and in Victoria, Australia. Sometimes it was the configuration of the pattern that suggested the name - Mountain Beech, Pineapple, Dandelion, Noughts and Crosses, Farm Gate, United and Mercury Energy being examples of this. Mrs Margaret Foster's work is acknowledged and where known the names she gave are used, this information is included with the stitch pattern charts and photographs (pages 34-64).

A rich source of patterns can be found in the flora and cultural heritage of the indigenous people of our various homelands. For New Zealanders inspiration can be found in the Tapa cloth of the Pacific people and in some woven borders on Maori cloaks, see Bibliography page 112.

WORK A PRACTICE SAMPLER:

To practice Wessex stitch patterns and colour and thread combinations, work a Practice Sampler. Choose a neutral coloured fabric with a thread count that is easy to see. Experiment with different types of thread and colour combinations with which you are unfamiliar. You may also like to try the suggested Stitch Patterns on various counts of linen or experiment with the patterns by working them over more or less threads. Your practice sampler will prove to be a valuable reference source for future projects. Mrs Foster strongly suggested that each person should stitch a sampler or 'example' as she named it, to become familiar with stitches and the patterns they can make.

COLOUR:

Wessex Stitchery is as much about the use of colour as it is about the use of stitch and pattern making. To gain the most benefit, think of your working sampler as a colour exercise as well as a method of recording patterns. Work the same pattern in different combinations: vary the emphasis by changing the dominant colour to the one used as a highlight, try cool colours, then warm tones.

HANDY HINT: Add a colour wheel to your thread collection, it is a very useful tool.

Look for colour combinations that interest you. Take your thread box out into the garden, find the colours to mix and blend by matching the beautiful unexpected colour schemes that just seem to happen in nature. Look closely into flowers, find the surprise accents, note the proportions of tone and the colours of the foliage. Record your findings with a small thread swatch. In the Millennium Sampler the colours are those of the perennial Cheiranthus, or variegated, perennial wallflower.

I store my threads by colour, not brand or number. With a full range of shades, tones and values in one place, on a 'palette' it does make it simpler to select colour schemes that please. Decide upon the 'main' thread colour, this will be influenced by the purpose of the project, colour of the linen or the lining fabric that you 'long' to use.

Place the 'main' coloured thread on the linen, if a lining has been selected, have it close by. Look first for similar colours that are close neighbours on the colour wheel, they may be warmer or cooler tones and a close value to the main colour. For the accent, find a colour that will 'sing'. It may be a complementary colour from the opposite side of the colour wheel. To find colour values see page 20. A few simple stitches give you the opportunity to create many different stitch patterns, remember to use variations in colour as well as stitch in your designs. This is the special joy of Wessex Stitchery.

HANDY HINT: When selecting colours, cut small lengths to lay on the fabric to ensure they create a pleasing combination. The white cards threads are wound on can be a distraction.

Interesting colour combinations can be found in:
Books on Embroidered Textiles i.e.
Treasures of the Embroiderers' Guild.
Stitch Magic - Jan Beaney & Jean Littlejohn.
Embroidery from Sketch to Stitch, Pat Langford.
Interior Decorating and Gardening Magazines
Geographical and Nature magazines
The world around us
Patterned fabrics.

When working a stitch pattern you may decide you wish to change the emphasis of the colours used. In the Melbourne panel page 80 the less dominant red and yellow, were used to keep the basic shape of the pattern working as the navy was changed to blue/gray and then to gray/green. Note how small amounts of the 'new' changing colours were introduced and blended into the composition. When changing one colour in a design you may find that other colours also need to be changed as the colour balance has been altered.

The two or three needle and thread method

Two or three threads, each threaded through its own needle and used separately can be used together most harmoniously in the two or three needle and thread method to give subtle colour variations in your work.

Use two or three threads from your selection or use one of the threads and then choose one or two more threads that are very close to it in value.

To stitch and blend colour with two or three threaded needles at a time:
• Keep the thread length short.
• To avoid tangles, keep all the needles and threads on the face of the work and 'park' the threaded needles away from the stitching, while awaiting their turn to be used.
• Work a few stitches with one colour, then change to another.
• Select which coloured thread to use in a random way.
• Enjoy. You will be well pleased with the effect.

This method of blending colour while stitching changes the total appearance of an embroidery, giving a much livelier look and adding another dimension to your work. A 'variegated' effect can be achieved that is more subtle than commercial or specially dyed threads and also gives you the freedom to choose just the colours you want to blend. It was used in the samplers in the patterns: Aspiring Tussock, Dunedin, Dunstan, Pembroke and Outram. The thread colour combinations are listed with each sampler.

To Determine Colour Values

To find threads that are the same value:

Twist two threads together i.e. a six strand of cotton with another six strand. Squint and scan, if they stripe they are not the same value, if they blend together so that each shade is not too distinct from the other, then you know that they are the same value or very similar.

To Enlarge or Reduce Stitch Patterns

It is simple to enlarge or reduce the size of the stitch patterns by either changing to a different linen count or increasing the thread count of the pattern. If the diagram shows a long tail chain with the head worked over two threads and the tail worked over six threads, enlarge it so the head is worked over three and the tail over nine threads. If you are unsure of the best size to work a pattern on a given piece of linen, stitch it in both sizes on the linen with the different threads you plan to use and decide which effect you like best.

General Points to Remember

- All stitches and stitch patterns may be varied in size.
- Stitches used in creating a given pattern are listed.
- Use a tapestry needle to establish the pattern, a crewel needle when the thread count is no longer applicable.
- It is recommended that you stitch these patterns in the order in which the stitches are listed at the end of each pattern.
- Use the suggestions as a guide only, they are not exhaustive.
- Fabric and Threads given are those used in the accompanying photograph.
- Use these notes as a guide only. Enjoy creating your own projects.

HANDY HINT: Remember to use a crewel needle when counting is not required and the needle is taken into the fabric not between the threads.

To Place Patterns

There is no need to spend time graphing out Wessex Stitchery patterns. Remember Mrs Foster's philosophy and method of working - pick up a needle and start stitching! With this in mind it is not necessary to slavishly copy, or worry over the placement of pattern and text. Wessex Stitchery is a joyous free counted thread technique that uses simple stitches to create diverse patterns and glorious colour. Spaces can always be filled with Narrow Borders. The following is a simple guide to placement of patterns:

- Tack over and under three or four threads to mark the centre vertically and horizontally (if required), choose the count that the pattern is divisible by and use that as your guide.
- Use the tacked centre as a guide for pattern placement.
- **For bands** the first pattern can be either centred over the vertical tacked line or worked directly beside it
- **For pattern blocks** centre the design on or beside the horizontal and vertical tacking lines
- **For frames** decide the approximate size of the frame, place the pattern band on or beside the vertical centre tacking line at the top edge of the 'frame' and work out from this position.

When placing patterns it matters not if you are a thread or two out in the count. When working the Otago 150th year sampler I had a space to fill and added a double row of wave stitch that formed diamonds along the left hand side of the first group of text, see colour photograph page 75. This not only solved my 'challenge' it also gave the opportunity to flow more of the gold thread through my composition.

When a pattern is being worked to form a frame for text, stitch the 'frame' first as the stitch pattern is harder to adjust than the text. The text can be made to 'fit in'. The amount of text depends upon the space available once the Wessex Stitchery frame has been worked. Choose text to fit within the frame.

Do not consider 'Out of Count' as a mistake, rather see it as 'A Golden Opportunity'. Try not to think of Wessex Stitchery as the usual type of counted thread technique because it is not. Rather see it as an opportunity that allows you to work and think about your embroidery in a very much freer manner. Wessex Stitchery pattern making with simple stitches and glorious colour is very seductive - enjoy it!

TEXT

Mrs Foster generally included text in her embroidery and this added to its charm. It particularly appeals to me and is a feature I hope you too will enjoy. There are many alphabet charts available in different embroidery books so only two options are included here:

ALPHABET I as seen on Mrs Foster's Melbourne Piece page 80.

ALPHABET II as seen on the Otago 150th, Braithwaite and Millennium samplers pages 75, 77 and 79. Note that the count changes within a letter between either one or two threads. I have found this a simpler method of working. Any alphabet you choose to work with can be adjusted: vary the threads the letters are worked over and vary the threads between each letter and word.

TO CENTRE TEXT

Do not graph your text out, bear in mind Mrs Foster's philosophy and her method of working. Do tack a central line over and under three or four threads, choosing the count that the stitch pattern you plan to use with your lettering is divisible by.

- Write your lettering out placing the words in lines as you think they will fit.

- Count the letters in each line allow for the space between each word. Each letter is usually worked over two threads with one or two threads between each letter, allow three to six threads between each word.

- Add up the letters and spaces, halve that number to find the centre.

- Begin the lettering at the centre marked by the vertical tacked line by working the *middle* letter in the *middle* line of text first. Complete the word or words to the right. Take the thread back under the stitching to the centre tacking and complete the line, by stitching the letters backwards towards the left.

Alphabet I
Mrs Foster's Alphabet

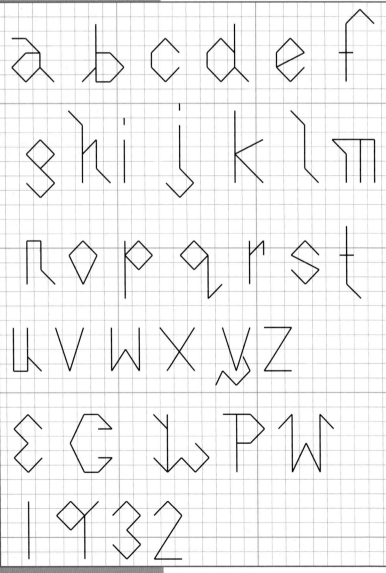

- The spacing does not need to be equal between each letter or between each word - fit in the words as you can.

- When placing text in a frame, embroider the frame first because most patterns are larger than is usual in a counted thread technique. (By working the other way it would be very easy to go beyond the space allowed for.)

- Find or Use text that will fit into the frame

Additional information on placing text as a band of pattern is given with the Samplers page 90.

FOR EXAMPLE A mighty -oak- is just a -little acorn -that stood -its ground could be counted and stitched like this.

*2+6+ **2**+2+**2**/+2+**2**+2+**2**+2+**2**+2+**2** =30*divide by 2 = 15
A   m   i / g   h   t   y

2+2+**2**=2=**2** =10 divide by 2 = 5
O/ak

2+2+**2**+6+**2**+2+**2**/+2+**2**+2+**2**+6+**2**=34 divide by 2=17
i   s   j   u / s   t   a

little / acorn 46
that / stood 38
its /ground 38

*numbers in bold relate to letters, the balance to the spaces between letters and words

- Start the embroidery by working the 'U' first, as it is the middle letter of the middle line of text. Complete the 'ST' leave six threads and work the 'A'. Take the thread back to the centre, work the 'J' leave the space - six threads and work 'IS'.

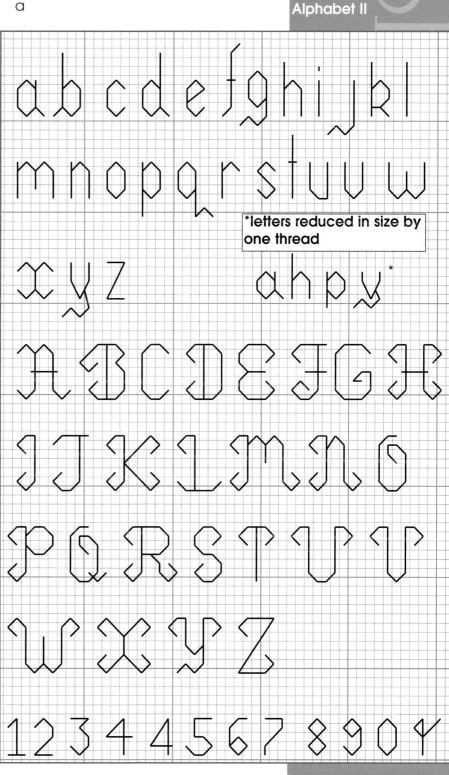

*letters reduced in size by one thread

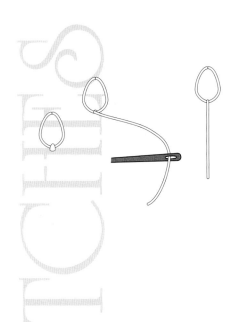

Chain Stitch - Short and Long Tail:

used frequently in Wessex Stitchery. The chain or 'head' is worked over a varying number of threads as is the anchoring straight stitch or 'tail'. The long tails are often pulled together and further embellished with wrapping, weaving, couching or interwoven with each other.

Couching:

used to underline lettering.

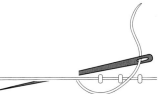

Fly Stitch -Long and Short Tail:

the head of fly stitch is worked over an even number of threads and is cleverly used to give a curved line or to 'draw' a pattern.

Herringbone:

used as a base to work chain stitch over, see Ritchie, a narrow border on the Melbourne panel

Needleweaving:

the thread weaves over and under stitches and is only attached at the beginning and end.

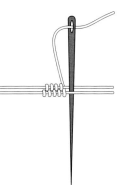

Overcast square:

so named by Mrs Foster, known in most recent stitch dictionaries as Algerian eye or eyelet stitch. Work over an even number of threads and always bring the needle out at the edge and take it down in the centre.

Straight stitch:

widely used for pattern making, to draw a line or fill a shape. Long stitches are held in place with a couched thread or back stitch as in Nigella and United. To bring in another colour, use straight stitch as a 'filling' stitch.

Wave stitch:

work from right to left over an even number of threads. Wave stitch is a good 'building block' for stitch pattern making; it can be stacked, made into diamonds and is useful for 'flowing' small amounts of colour through a composition.

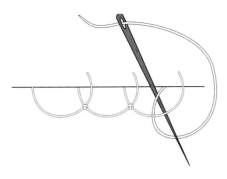

*Antwerp knotted buttonhole stitch:

a very useful edging stitch which is worked from left to right.

*Double Running Stitch:

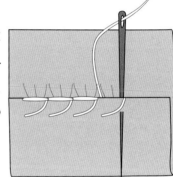

stitch from right to left over and under the same number of threads then turn and work from left to right over and under the same number of threads filling in the spaces.

*Ladder stitch:

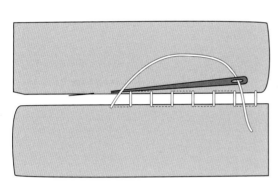

ideal for construction projects as it gives invisible fabric joins. The needle slides the length required within the fold of the fabric and is then taken straight across to the other side, inserted into the fold to slide along the length required, repeat. Pull to close the edges together once two to three stitches have been made.

*Hem stitch:

hold the work with the folded hem edge towards you. Gather two, three or four threads into the hem stitching as you prefer, then take the needle down between the linen and hem fold to catch a two thread deep section of the fold.

Back stitch:

used to make patterns; underline lettering; outline shapes; to flow contrasting colour and give added interest.

Back stitch spider's web:

work over a foundation of 'spokes' or around the long tails of fly or chain stitches.

Detached buttonhole:

work over laid threads and only anchor into the fabric to start and finish.

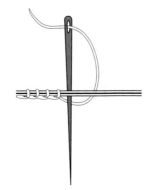

Buttonhole:

work from left to right.

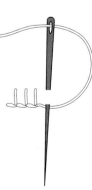

*STITCHES USED IN CONSTRUCTION

NEEDLECASE, PIN CUSHION AND SCISSOR TAG

Refer to colour photograph page 73

This little set of needlework accessories would make a charming gift for someone special or would be an attractive addition to your own collection. I used eight different colours to create the rich, stained glass effect with the pattern, Wanaka Maze. Each of the accessories has Wanaka Maze on the front, with the pincushion and needle case having different patterns on the reverse. This is a most enjoyable way to try out the many different patterns illustrated in this book. Either work each piece in the colours suggested, or have fun choosing and blending new colours, see page 17 for more information on colour selection.

PLEASE NOTE: When working a different Stitch Pattern, or using a different linen allow extra fabric and remember to include seam allowances. Begin the embroidery at the tacked centre of the main piece, complete all the stitch pattern blocks to establish the finished size before tacking the reverse side and hem allowance.

Requirements

- Linen: 32 count Belfast (colour 53) dark ecru 30 x 20 cm (12 x 8"). In these accessories the Wanaka Maze design is worked over an 18 thread block so although the linen may be finer than you are used to, you are working on a larger scale than in many other types of stitching.
- Lining: 11.5 x 18 cm (4 1/2 x 7")
- Flannel: 16cm x 10 cm (6 1/4 x 4")
- Filling: A large handful of dacron filling for pincushion
- Cord (1 m or 1 yd) to cover the join and add a loop on the pincushion and the loop on the scissors tag see page 103 for how to make finger cord.
- Needles: Tapestry sizes 24 - 26 and crewel needles sizes 5 - 8
- Threads as listed:

DMC No. 8 Perle cotton or stranded cottons 930 dark blue, 992 sea green, 597 pale teal, 3830 brick, 3826 ginger*, 437 pale apricot*, 320 green*, 368 pale green*.

Use two threads of 437 but for all other stranded cottons use three threads.

DMC 642 No 12 Perle for the Hemstitch,

DMC No 8 Perle ecru or stranded cotton colour of your choice for edging the flannel pages

*indicates DMC threads colours substituted for Anchor colours, 365, 568, 215, 216 which were used in the embroidery.

Wanaka Maze page 52, Melbourne page 42 and Dandelion page 35.

Wanaka Maze is stitched over an 18 x 18 thread block. The long tailed chain is worked with the 'head' over three threads and the 'tail' over six threads.

To prepare the linen:

Tack the outline of the needle case, pincushion and scissor tag following the layout diagram using the measurements given. Neaten the edge of the linen before you start to sew, for more information on this see page 14.

Embroider all designs before cutting them out, otherwise the fabric pieces are too small to handle comfortably. Neaten all raw edges once the embroidery is completed and the pieces have been cut out.

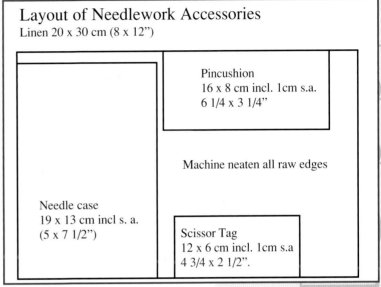

Layout of Needlework Accessories
Linen 20 x 30 cm (8 x 12")

Pincushion
16 x 8 cm incl. 1cm s.a.
6 1/4 x 3 1/4"

Machine neaten all raw edges

Needle case
19 x 13 cm incl s. a.
(5 x 7 1/2")

Scissor Tag
12 x 6 cm incl. 1cm s.a
4 3/4 x 2 1/2".

Needle case

Finished size 9.5 x 7.5 cm (3 3/4 x 3")
Front pattern: Wanaka Maze
Back pattern: Melbourne
Refer to the layout diagram for the needle case and tack where indicated, noting the number of threads to leave between each line of hem tacking. Remember all tacking is to be taken out to the edge of the linen. For more information on tacking see page 14.

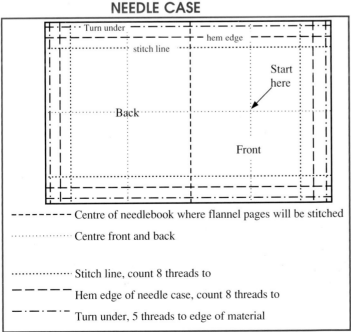

NEEDLE CASE

Turn under
hem edge
stitch line
Start here
Back
Front

------- Centre of needlebook where flannel pages will be stitched

·········· Centre front and back

·········· Stitch line, count 8 threads to

— — — Hem edge of needle case, count 8 threads to

—·—·— Turn under, 5 threads to edge of material

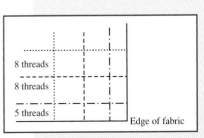

8 threads
8 threads
5 threads
Edge of fabric

To Stitch The Front

Work the pattern Wanaka Maze twelve times, (4 rows of 3 patterns). Start at the centre front of the needlebook and move out from there, see diagram. Complete all the first stage of the pattern before moving on to stages II, III and IV.

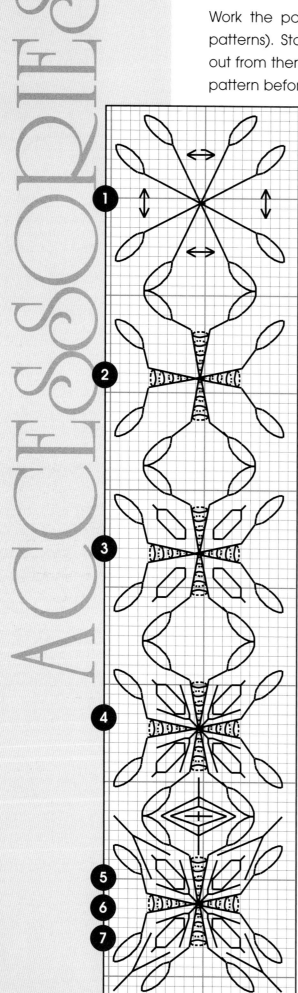

STAGE 1 is worked using a tapestry needle and dark blue.

The long tailed chain is worked with the 'head' over three threads and the 'tail' over six threads, for a block 18 x 18 threads.

STAGE 2 still using the dark blue thread and a tapestry needle wrap the tails together (approx. 5 - 7 wraps). Begin at the centre and wrap towards the chain stitch head. Refer to stitch pattern, arrows indicate which threads are to be wrapped together.
The rest of Wanaka Maze Pattern is worked using a crewel needle.

STAGE 3 Chain stitch with brick is worked in the spaces between the wrapped tails.

STAGE 4 Work fly stitch with green between the wrapped tails and the head of the brick coloured chain stitch.

STAGE 5 Using ginger work fly stitch around the tail of the brick chain stitch.

STAGE 6 Fly stitch filling - to give a glow vary the colours, Sea green, Pale teal.

STAGE 7 Work a straight stitch where indicated using pale green, it is couched within the fly stitch filling.

STAGE 8 Optional - use pale apricot and work fly stitch around the tails of some of the brick coloured chain stitches. It is used as a highlight only refer to photograph page 53 for its placement.

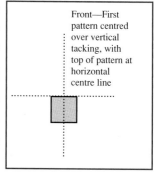

Front—First pattern centred over vertical tacking, with top of pattern at horizontal centre line

The verse, *a stitch in time,* is worked over three threads, three threads beyond the edge of 'Wanaka Maze' on the front of the needlecase. Centre the verse on each side of the pattern. I used Alphabet II given on page 23. For placement of text refer to page 22.

The pattern on the reverse of the needlebook is 'Melbourne' see page 42. It is stitched using dark blue thread throughout. To frame the quote *'a stitch in time'* the chain stitch portion of the Melbourne stitch pattern has been placed on each of the four sides, refer to diagram for its placement. I then worked three rows of couching to join the blocks of chain stitch and added my name and the date beneath this.

HANDY HINT: I always work the 'frame' first then fit in the message as it is easier to adjust text than a stitch pattern.

On completion of all the embroidery cut the needle case out and neaten the edges in the usual way. The needle case has a hemmed edge with mitred corners. With your tacked lines as a guide mitre the corners and hem the edges. See page 101 for how to mitre a corner and page 25 for hemstitch.

When you have completed the hem work a row of wave stitch (see page 24) just inside the hemline. Fold the raw edges of the lining to fit within the hem stitch and slip stitch the lining to the hem stitching.

FLANNEL PAGES: Cut the flannel 2 cm (3/4") larger than the required finished size of the pages of 14 x 8 cms (5½ x 3¼) . To mark the finished size withdraw one thread on each side. It will also give a channel to work into and a cutting guide when the stitching is complete. With matching No 8 Perle thread, work buttonhole stitches between each thread and over three or four fabric threads, right round the edge of the 'page'. Because both sides of the 'page' are seen, start and finish threads by darning them into the weave of the flannel at the corners (which strengthens them) and cover with stitching. When the stitching is complete carefully clip the extra fabric away from beside the stitching. This method of working ensures nice flat 'pages' without wavy edges!

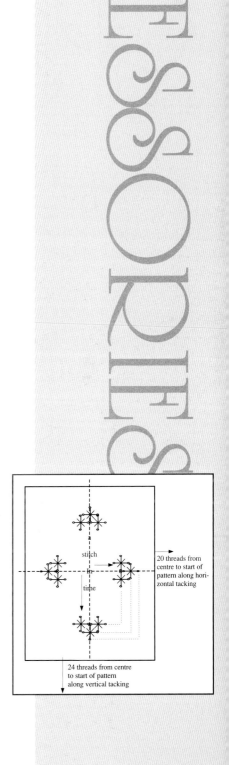

stitch

in

time

20 threads from centre to start of pattern along horizontal tacking

24 threads from centre to start of pattern along vertical tacking

Attach the flannel page by working double running stitch (see page 25) along the centre tacked line, taking care to position the stitching accurately through all layers. You may need to guide the exit of the needle with your fingers to ensure it comes out in the correct position. Finish with a row of wave stitch worked either side of the double running stitch. It is worked into the linen only, do not catch the lining.

Pincushion

Finished size 6 cm square (2 1/4" sq)
Front Pattern: Wanaka Maze worked over 18 threads
Back Pattern: Dandelion page 35

Refer to the layout guide for the pin cushion and tack where indicated, for more information on the correct way to tack see page 14.

Starting at the centre work nine Wanaka Maze pattern repeats (three rows of three) using the same threads and in the same order as it was stitched in the Needle case. This will be the front of your Pincushion.

For the back of your Pincushion centre the 'Dandelion' stitch pattern and work once. It is worked using dark blue throughout. Work your initials within the centre of the Dandelion pattern and the year on the outer edge.

Cut the pincushion pieces out, neaten the raw edges and fold down 1 cm (1/2") hem allowance on each side of each piece, mitre the corners see diagram and tack to hold in place. (It is better to mitre the corners of these small items as it makes the corners less bulky.)

Fold down corner and tack in place.

To make up the pincushion:

With wrong sides together ladder stitch (see page 25) the front and back of the pincushion together leaving part of the fourth side open to insert the filling. Push the filling into the corners, a stiletto makes this easier or a little filling stitched into the corners will also help. Once firmly filled ladder stitch the fourth side closed. Attach a cord over the join, making a loop at the corners if desired. A 30 cm (12") cord is required. To make a finger cord 120cm (48") of stranded cotton (DMC 930) or No. 8 Perle is required, see page 103 for instructions.

Pincushion
16 x 8 cm incl. 1cm s.a.
6 1/4 x 3 1/4"

To attach the cord to the pincushion use a crewel needle and one thread of stranded cotton the same colour as the cord. To keep the nice shape of the cord, take the needle and thread through the cord and into the seam line of the pin cushion.

...... Tack 1 cm (1/2") s.a. turn down hem along this line

---- Tack to mark centre front and back

Solid line indicates edge of each pattern piece. Cut along these lines on completion of all embroidery.

— — Fold to mitre corners along these lines

HANDY HINT: If using fleece make a cloth inner bag to hold the filling.

Finished Size 4cm square (1 5/8" sq)

Stitch Pattern: same front and back, Wanaka Maze, worked over 18 threads.

To prepare the linen:

Refer to the layout guide for the Scissors Tag and tack where indicated. For more information on the correct way to tack see page 14.

Starting at the centre work four repeats of the pattern Wanaka Maze on each side of the scissors tag as before.

Joining and finishing:

On completion of the embroidery cut out the pieces and machine neaten the cut edges. Fold down edges 1cm, (1/2"), mitre corners and tack in place. Make or buy a cord 30 cm (12") long. To make a finger cord use stranded cotton DMC 930 or No 8 Perle 120cm (48") long, see page 103.

Attach the two raw ends of the cord to a corner on the wrong side of the scissors tag using the short ends at the start of the finger cord or three threads of stranded cotton if using bought cord. With the wrong sides together, join the edges by working buttonhole stitch one thread apart and three threads deep around all four sides, stitching firmly through the cord at the corner using the long threads at the end of the finger cord or three threads of DMC 930 stranded or No 8 Perle.

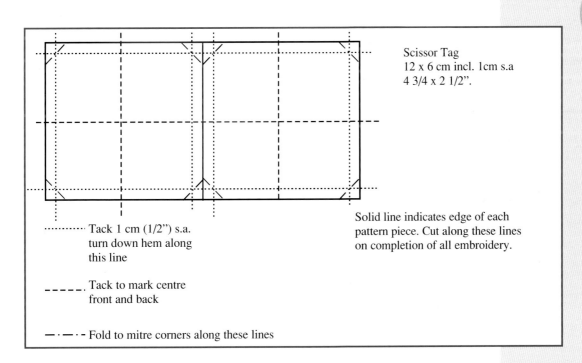

Scissor Tag
12 x 6 cm incl. 1cm s.a
4 3/4 x 2 1/2".

Solid line indicates edge of each pattern piece. Cut along these lines on completion of all embroidery.

·············· Tack 1 cm (1/2") s.a. turn down hem along this line

— — — —. Tack to mark centre front and back

— · — · · Fold to mitre corners along these lines

TRAY CLOTH

Finished size 44 x 29 cm (17 x 11 1/2")
Refer to colour photograph page 76

A beautifully embroidered tray cloth to use with your best china will add a special touch to any occasion. It would make a very distinguished wedding or birthday gift especially if the pattern and colours were chosen to compliment the recipient's tea set and furnishings. Matching little afternoon tea napkins, with the embroidery in one corner, would make this even more illustrious. Gifts of embroidery that have been especially designed for the occasion or purpose become an important reminder of a valued friendship. Such pieces are a memorable gift from grandparents to their grandchildren and become family heirlooms. Your beautiful work will tell future generations a great deal about you. Select linen to match the china, a pattern that appeals to you and embroider it in the colours you enjoy. You will not be disappointed.

There are a number of stitch patterns that would be ideal for further table linen projects. I would like to make a set of luncheon mats using the same coloured threads, but each mat would be worked in a different stitch pattern or combination of patterns. It would be a good conversation piece as guests would compare the patterns before them. For table mats, I would place the embroidery on the left hand side and for napkins I would work a corner motif only.

Requirements

- Fabric: Glenshee Linen 28 count, colour pale grey 50cm x 35cm (20 x 14"). For alternative linen and threads refer to page 11.
- Threads as listed:
DMC stranded cottons: 3041 Antique lilac 3 skeins, 676 butter 1 skein, 367 medium green 2 skeins.
Two threads of stranded cotton were used at all times.

Stitch pattern:

Lindisfarne I - Pattern repeat every 24 threads, see page 39

To prepare the linen

Machine neaten the edges before you start to stitch, see before you begin page 14.
Start working the stitch pattern at one corner 5 cm (2") in from each edge and stitch the length required. To ensure accurate placement of the pattern you may find it helpful to tack over

and under four threads to mark the *centre* of the design. The pattern is easy to work round a corner, refer to the photograph for additional detail.

As the tray cloth will be viewed from each side take special care to keep the back of the work as tidy as possible, use option 2 page 15 to start a new thread. Finish old threads by taking them under the overcast square to secure firmly.

TRAY CLOTH LAYOUT

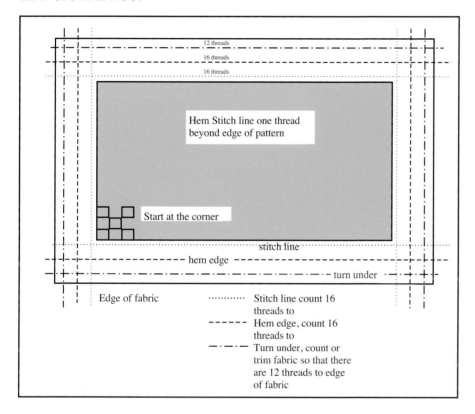

The Hem

This cloth has a (1.2 cm 1/2" or 16 thread deep) hem with mitred corners and is stitched just one thread beyond the edge of the design. To stitch the hem follow the instructions for hems and mitred corners page 101. Allowing 16 threads between the 'stitch line' and 'hem edge' and between the hem edge and 'turn under'. Allow 12 threads between the 'turn under' and neatened edge of the fabric. It is stitched in place using hem stitch worked over every two threads, see page 25.

Because I did not want the hem stitching to intrude upon the pattern, I used threads withdrawn from the linen for this purpose. Use a fairly short linen thread, it may need to be twisted as you work.

Do remember to work your name and date on the reverse side of the hem.

Congratulations you have completed a beautiful piece of heritage embroidery that will become a family heirloom.

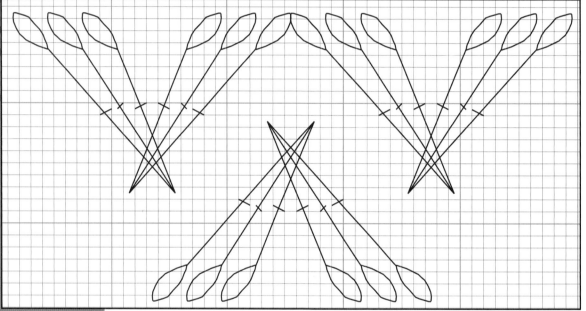

BENDIGO: Pattern No 12 'Embroidery' Vol. 11 No. 3 June 1934.

At a class taught in Bendigo, the students said the shape of this stitch pattern reminded them of the 'Poppets', structures seen in their very rich Australian gold mining region.

STITCHES: Long tail chain, couched in place

USE: in blocks, bands or borders.

OPTION: change the scale - work the head and tail over a different numbers of threads

ORDER OF WORKING: Long tail chain, couching

Photograph: Fabric: Lugana. 25 count Threads: DMC No 8 Perle 3041

DANDELION: from Mrs Foster's May 1918 sampler

STITCHES: Overcast square and straight, note the varying length of the straight stitches

USE: in blocks, bands or borders

OPTION: change the scale, reduce each stitch by one thread, centre can be filled

ORDER OF WORKING: overcast square red, straight stitches blue

Photograph: Fabric: cotton 28 count. Threads DMC stranded, two threads 931, one thread 919.

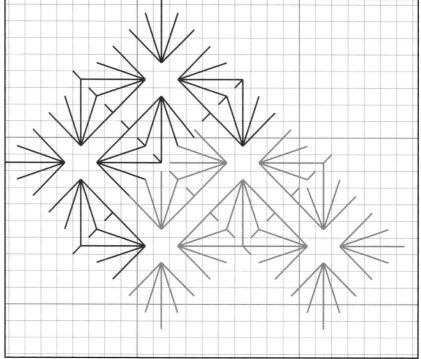

Notches indicate end of stitches.

DUNEDIN: Mrs Foster's May 1918 Sampler

Named for Dunedin (Gaelic for Edinburgh), my home city, which is encircled with a 200ha belt of untouched native bush. This reserve was left by the pioneers to remind future generations of the appearance of the land on their arrival in 1848. Used in the Otago Sampler page 75 and Braithwaite Sampler page 79.

STITCHES: straight

USE: in blocks, bands, borders or as single units

OPTION: colour blend with two or three needles and threads

Photograph: Fabric: Edinburgh 35 count linen. Threads: stranded cottons, one thread of DMC 931 and Anchor 876 - worked with two needles and threads.

DUNSTAN: from 'Embroidery' Vol. 23 No.1 Spring 1972 (variation)

Mrs Foster considered that Saint Dunstan inspired and encouraged British embroiderers.

STITCHES: fly, straight and long tail chain

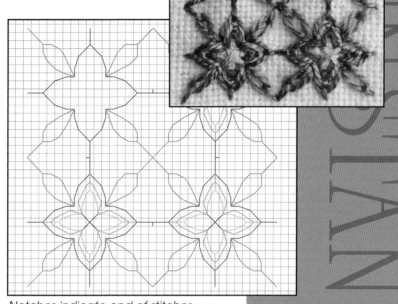

USE: in blocks, bands or borders

ORDER OF WORKING: Fly red, yellow, change to a sharp needle to work orange fly stitches between the red and yellow fly stitches. Straight blue, Long tail chain green.

Photograph Fabric: cotton 28 count. Threads: DMC No 8 Perle 931, 932, stranded two threads of 3778, 676, 905.

Notches indicate end of stitches.

DUNSTAN TRAIL: Stitch 3 'Embroidery' Vol. 11 No. 3 June 1934.

This design looks like wagon wheels, and reminded me of the route taken to the Central Otago gold fields in the eighteen sixties.

STITCHES: straight and detached buttonhole

USE: in blocks, bands, borders or as single units see Abbie's Memory Pocket page 74.

OPTION: Change the colours used for the detached buttonhole, to give a floral effect.

ORDER OF WORKING: Straight stitches blue, red, weave gold thread three times under and over the blue straight stitches (the 'spokes'), where indicated by the orange line, to form a circle. (The weaving is over the straight 'spokes' and under on the diagonal.) Then work Detached Buttonhole over the woven circle, as each new 'spoke' is reached catch it in the buttonhole stitching to stabilise. To start detached buttonhole bring the needle out to the left of one of the 'spokes'.

Photograph: Fabric: Lugana 25 count.
Threads: DMC stranded two threads of 436

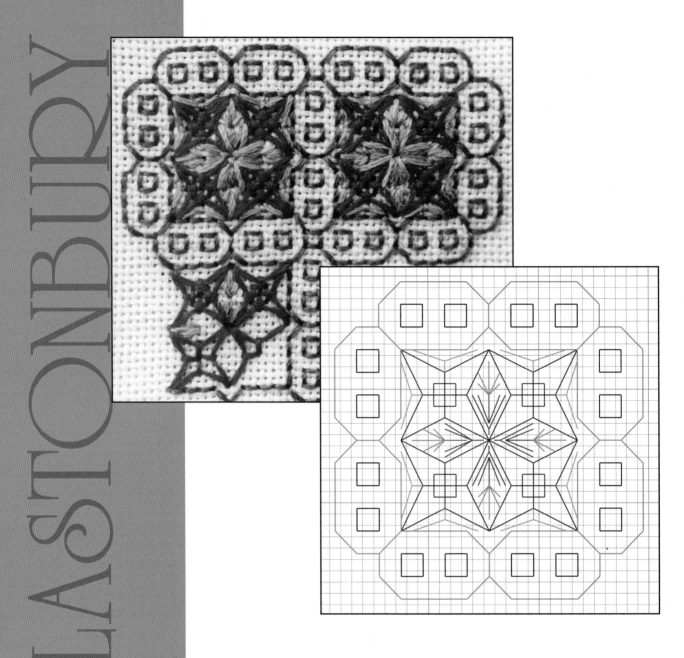

GLASTONBURY: from 'Embroidery' Vol. 23 No. 1 Spring 1972

Named for Glastonbury Abbey, a Christian sanctuary of Wessex so ancient that only legend can record its origin.

STITCHES: fly, straight and back stitch

USE: in blocks, bands or borders. Increase the scale or use 18 - 20 count linen and work in wool for a cushion cover.

OPTION: Instead of the straight stitch filling; work a chain stitch and fill its centre with a small straight stitch

ORDER OF WORKING: Back stitch over two threads green, Straight stitch squares red, Fly stitch blue, Straight stitch over fly stitch red, Fly stitch deep green, Straight stitch wine and yellow, Fly stitch mauve.

Photograph: Fabric: Lugana 25 count. Threads: DMC stranded two threads 930, 931, 355, 833 and 581.

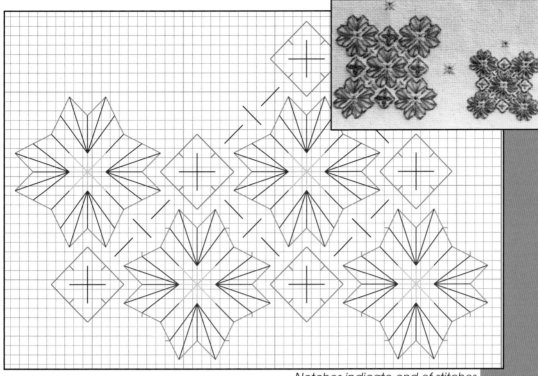

Notches indicate end of stitches.

LINDISFARNE I: Stitch 7 'Embroidery' Vol. 11 No. 3 June 1934.

See Otago 150th sampler page 75 and Tray cloth page 76.

STITCHES: straight, overcast square, back - option chain stitch

USE: in blocks, bands or borders.

OPTION: Note scale options shown in photographs. The straight stitches inside the back stitch squares can be replaced with detached chain stitches.

ORDER OF WORKING: Overcast square yellow, Straight stitch red, Back stitch over two threads orange, Back stitch over two threads green. Straight stitch blue

Photograph: Fabric: Cotton 28 count. Threads: Purple option DMC No. 8 Perle 3041, 676, 937, Anchor stranded cotton three threads 876. Pink option DMC No. 8 Perle 223, 435, 676, 320 Anchor stranded three threads 876. Blue option: Fabric: Linen 20 count, Threads: No 8 Perle DMC 783, 992, Anchor 0281, 0158.

From Otago Sampler page 75

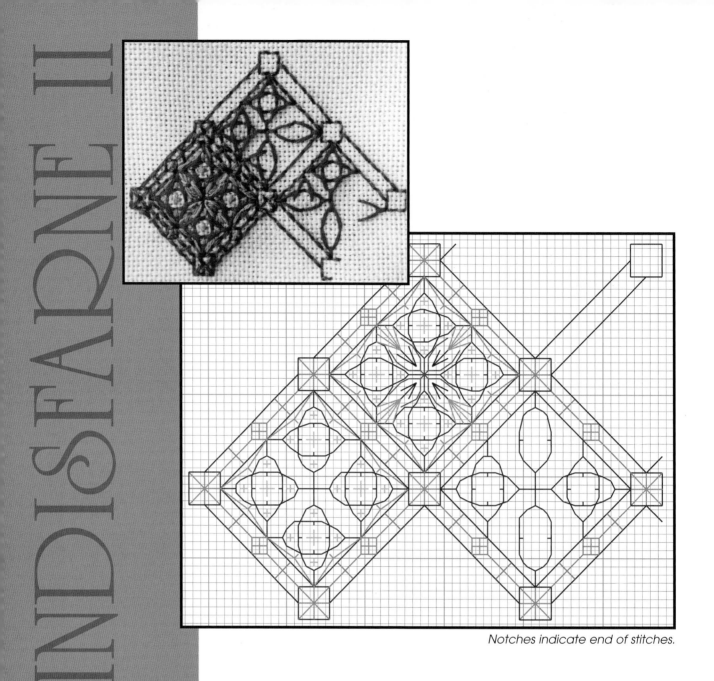

Notches indicate end of stitches.

LINDISFARNE II: from Melbourne Panel page 80

STITCHES: back, long tail fly and straight

USE: in blocks, bands, increase the scale or use 18 - 20 count linen and work in wool for a cushion cover.

OPTION: fill shapes with chain stitches instead of the straight stitches.

ORDER OF WORKING: Back stitch over two threads blue, Straight stitch bright green, Overcast square and straight stitches orange, Fly stitch red, Straight stitch yellow, Change to a crewel needle to work further stitches - Fly stitch gray, Straight stitch purple, mauve, Fly stitch light green

Photograph : Fabric: Lugana 25 count. Threads: DMC stranded two threads 501, 3830, 734, 930.

MARGARET STITCH: Stitch 10 'Embroidery' Vol. 11 No. 3 June 1934

Named by Mrs Foster and used in 'The Buttercup Meadow' and 'Poppy Patch' Hussifs see page 78.

STITCHES: Long tail chain with optional needleweaving.

USE: in blocks or bands

OPTIONS: Long tail chain with either a head of two or three threads and tail of six or nine threads respectively. Needle weave over each group of three long tails as seen on the hussifs. Mrs Foster used this pattern without the needleweaving. See alternate sizing page 84.

ORDER OF WORKING: Long tail chain then needleweaving

Photograph: Fabric: Lugana 25 count. Threads: DMC No 8 Perle 320, With needleweaving, DMC No 8 Perle 315, 436

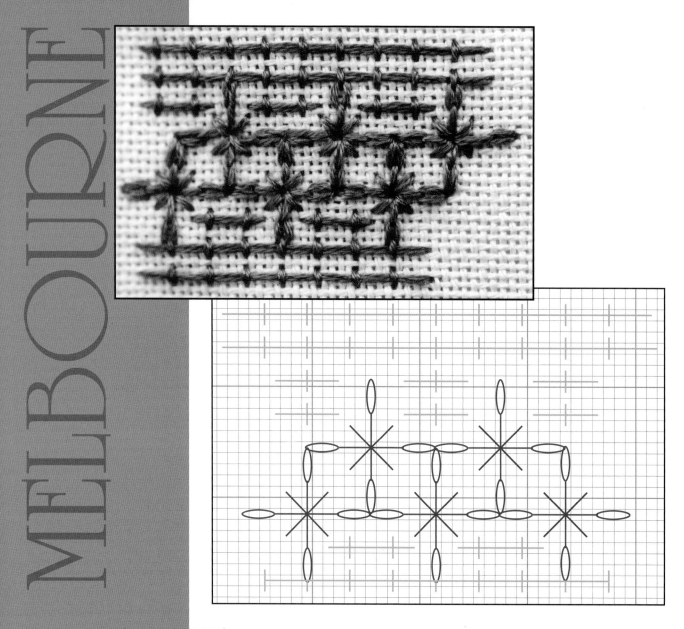

MELBOURNE: from 'Embroidery' Vol. 23, No.1 Spring 1972

Not named by Mrs Foster but named Melbourne, for its wide, tree canopied, tram lined streets.

STITCHES: straight, long tail chain, and couching

USE: in blocks, bands or borders
In this pattern the Long Tail Chain stitch becomes part of an overcast square.

OPTION: Alter the placement of 'trees 'and 'tram lines' Use three threads to stitch the 'trees' and two threads for the 'tramlines'

ORDER OF WORKING: Long tail chain red, Straight stitch green, Couching gold

Photograph: Fabric: Lugana 25 count Threads: DMC stranded three threads 3041

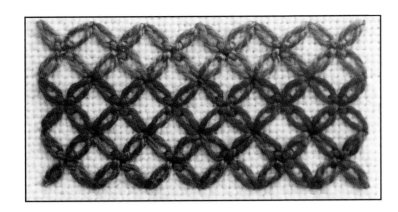

MERCURY ENERGY: Stitch 4 'Embroidery' Vol. 11 No. 3 June 1934

Not named by Mrs Foster

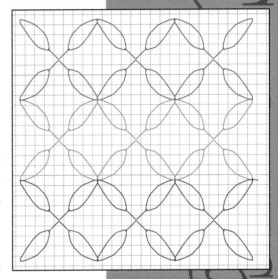

STITCH: detached chain

USE: in blocks, bands, borders or as individual units

OPTION: Change scale - chain stitch head over two, three or four threads, tail over one thread or as required. Grade colour as shown; add a cross stitch or similar to the voided centres, increase the number of rows.

Photograph: Fabric: Cotton 28 count. Threads: DMC No 8 Perle 3328, 355, 315.

MOUNTAIN BEECH: Stitch 9 from 'Embroidery' Vol. 11 No. 3 June 1934

Used on the reverse of Taylor Memory Pocket page 71 not shown in photograph

STITCHES: overcast square, detached chain

USE: in blocks, bands, or build up a pattern by stacking, half drops, or bricking.

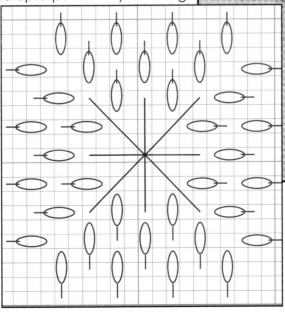

OPTION: Blocks can be worked side by side, or separated by two, three, or four fabric threads

ORDER OF WORKING: Overcast square blue, Detached chain red

Photograph: Fabric: Cotton 28 count. Threads: DMC No 8 Perle 436

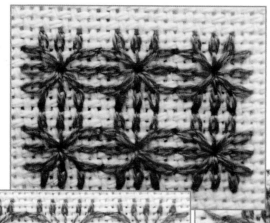

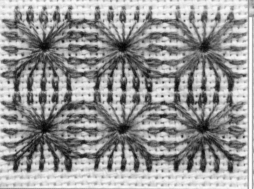

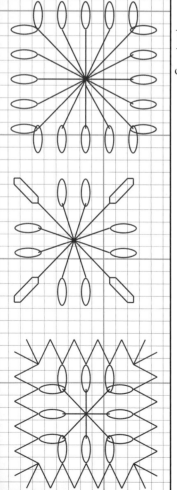

MRS FOSTER: Stitch 14 'Embroidery' Vol. 11 No. 3 June 1934

'Embroidery' 1934 listed this Stitch Pattern as a favourite of Mrs Foster and I have named it in her honour.

STITCHES: Long tail chain. Use fine thread i.e. one thread of stranded cotton, otherwise it is too bulky. *Note at each corner there are either two stitches with the head of the chain angled in two directions or one chain stitch head on the diagonal*

USE: in blocks, bands, spots, borders, or build up a pattern by stacking or bricking.

OPTION: surround the squares with either wave or detached chain. Each block could be worked right up to its neighbour, or could be separated by two, three or four fabric threads. It can be enlarged as required

ORDER OF WORKING: Long tail chain blue, Wave stitch red

Photograph: Fabric: Lugana 25 count. Threads: DMC stranded one thread 3830.

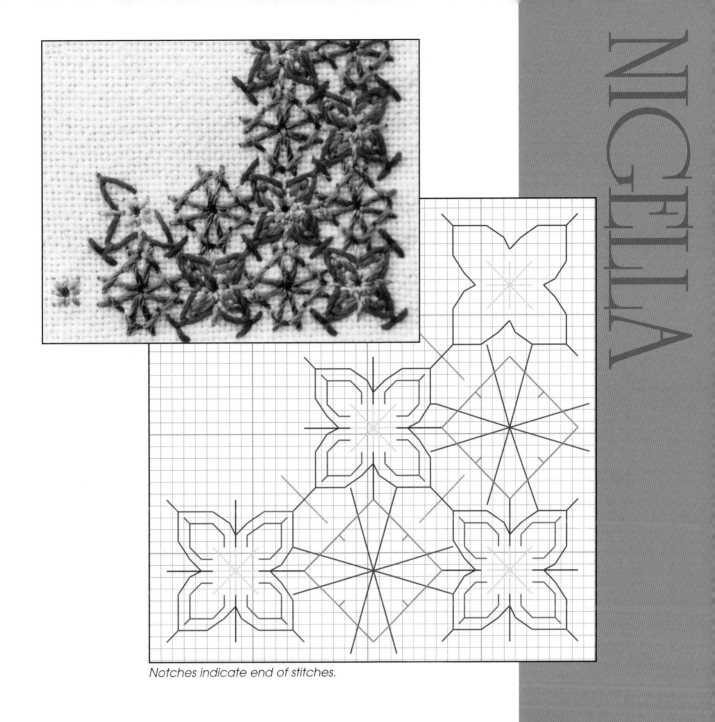

Notches indicate end of stitches.

NIGELLA: Stitch 8 'Embroidery' Vol. 11 No. 3 June 1934

See Millennium sampler page 77.

STITCHES: Overcast square, fly, detached chain, straight and back stitches

USE: in blocks, bands or borders.

ORDER OF WORKING: Overcast square yellow, Fly red, gray, Straight dark green, Back stitch worked over three threads light green, Straight stitch purple, orange. Use a crewel needle when you are no longer able to work to a thread count yet want to fit further stitches and colour into the stitch pattern.

Photograph: Fabric: Cotton 28 count, Threads: No 8 Perle DMC 355, 783, 937, Anchor 0356, 0281.

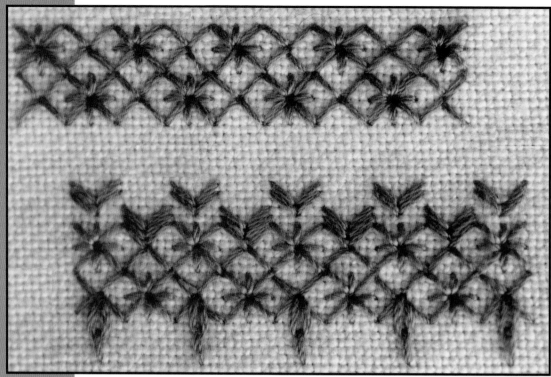

Original

Variation

NOUGHTS & CROSSES:
Stitch 6 'Embroidery' Vol. 11 No. 3 June 1934

Used on the reverse of 'The Buttercup Meadow' and 'Poppy Patch' hussifs but not shown in photograph.

STITCHES: Overcast square and back stitch

USE: in blocks, bands or borders.

OPTION: add fly, long tail chain and/or wave stitches. Work the overcast square in a variety of shades to look like flowers, see the hussifs. As with all Wessex Stitch Patterns the possible variations are limitless!

ORDER OF WORKING: Overcast square red, Straight or back stitch blue, Wave stitch green, Chain yellow

Photograph: Fabric: Cotton 28 count. Threads DMC No 8 Perle 320, variation 320, 436

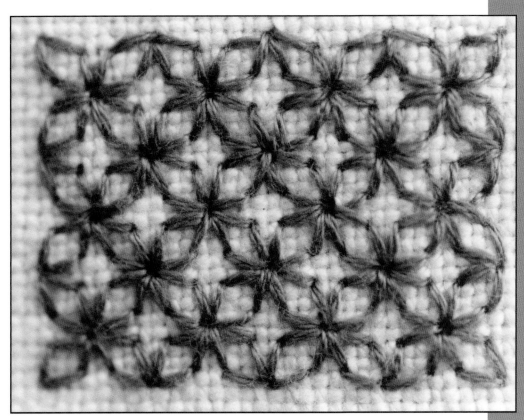

OUTRAM: from Mrs Foster's May 1918 Sampler

Outram named for a pleasant glen, which is a local picnic spot. See Otago 150th Sampler Page 75 and Braithwaite sampler page 79.

STITCHES: back stitch worked over three or more threads

USE: in blocks, bands or as a narrow border fill in. A single pattern can be used to decorate the beginning of a sentence, see Otago 150th sampler.

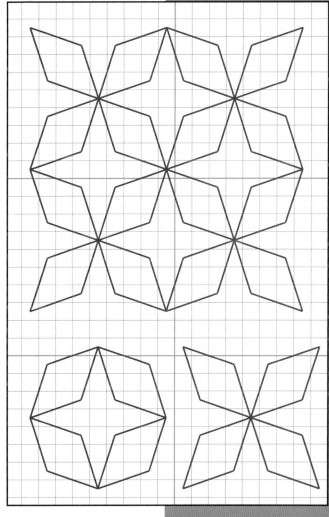

OPTION: This pattern is ideal for the two or three needle and thread technique using threads with a close colour value. Change arrangement of diamonds, see chart.

Photograph: Fabric: Edinburgh Linen 35 count. Threads: Stranded one thread of DMC 931 and Anchor 876.

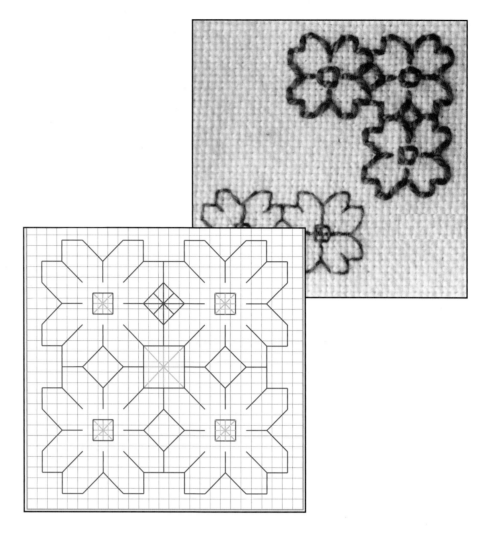

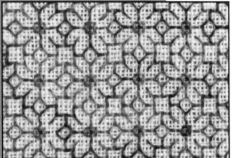

**From Braithwaite Sampler
page 79**

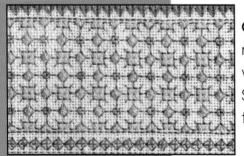

**From Otago Sampler
page 75 (variation)**

PEMBROKE: from Mrs Foster's May 1918 Sampler

The name for this pattern was inspired by the wonderful wild flowers which grow in Wanaka, in the park of this name, and throughout the Central Otago Lakes District.

STITCHES: Back stitch over two, three or four threads

USE: either in blocks, bands or borders.

OPTION: fill the void between each floret with square rounds see Otago 150th Sampler. To 'variegate' the colour, work with three needles and threads see Braithwaite Sampler. For more information on colour blending with three needles see page 19.

ORDER OF WORKING: Back stitch over two threads as shown or three or four threads red, Overcast square yellow, Square round can be added green.

Photograph: Fabric: Cotton 28 count. Threads: Two unit example one thread of DMC stranded 356, Three unit example DMC No 8 Perle 3328

PINEAPPLE: stitch 11 'Embroidery' Vol. 11 No. 3 June 1934

See the Taylor Memory Pocket page 74

STITCHES: Overcast square variation note the extra long stitches must be worked twice to support needleweaving.

USE: in blocks, bands or borders.
The needleweaving is worked in the threads only except at the beginning and end when it is taken into the fabric to stabilise the design.

OPTION: enlarge or reduce the scale, work needleweaving in either short bands or square blocks.

ORDER OF WORKING: Overcast square blue, Needleweaving red

Photograph: Fabric: Lugana 25 count. Threads DMC No 8 Perle 931

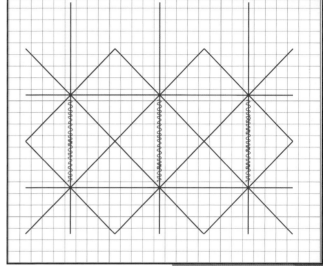

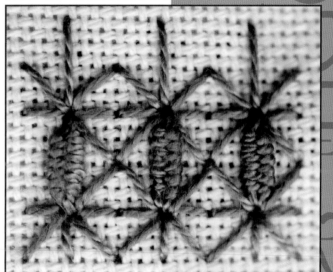

RITCHIE: from the Melbourne Panel page 80

STITCHES: Herringbone, chain or raised chain band, or raised stem band.

USE: in bands and borders.

OPTION: Work herringbone the depth required.

ORDER OF WORKING: Herringbone green, Chain stitch red - worked over the herringbone stitch and not into the fabric except at beginning and end of stitching.

Photograph: Fabric: Lugana 25 count. Threads DMC No. 8 Perle 436, 3041, 315

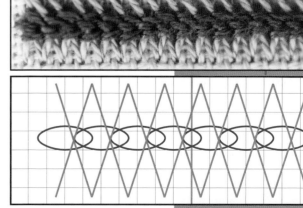

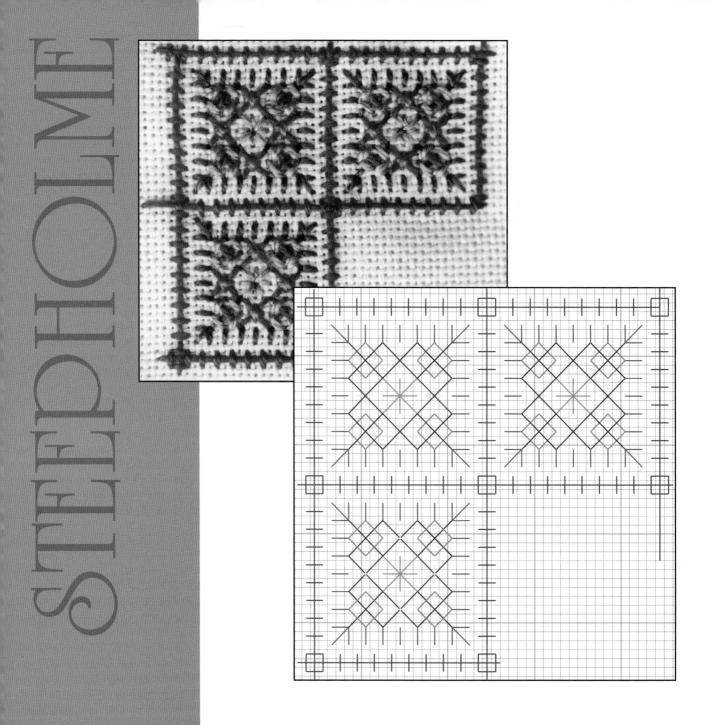

STEEPHOLME: from 'Embroidery' Vol. 23 No. 1 Spring 1972

STITCHES: Straight and couching.

USE: in blocks, bands or borders.

OPTION: work in wool on 18 - 20 even weave fabrics for cushion covers

ORDER OF WORKING: Straight or back stitch red, straight stitch blue, light green, yellow, Overcast square mustard, Straight stitch gray, Couching (outer edge) green

Photograph: Fabric: Lugana 25 count. Threads DMC: No 8 Perle 315, 355, 3328, 436 and three threads stranded 581.

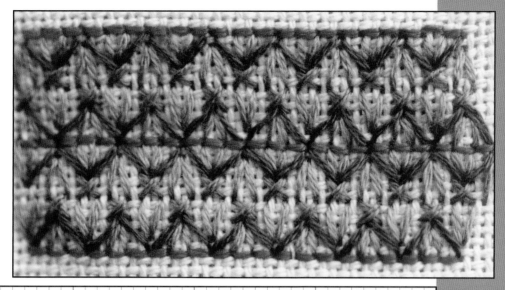

VICTORIA: from Melbourne Panel page 80

STITCHES: wave, cross, back

USE: in blocks or bands see Melbourne panel where the quotation is stitched into the narrow bands.

ORDER OF WORKING: Back stitch over two threads red, Wave stitch blue, individual wave stitches gold, Cross stitch green (note how the cross stitch is snug to the top of the wave)

Photograph: Fabric: Lugana 25 count. Threads DMC stranded two threads 930, 931, 581 and 3328.

WANAKA MAZE: 'Embroidery' Vol. 11 No. 3 June 1934 (variation).

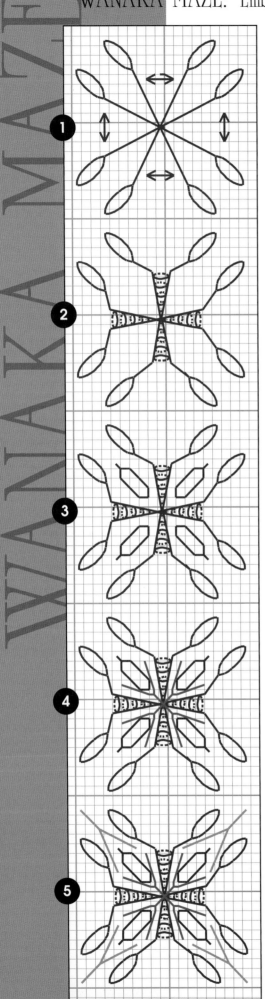

Named because it is hard to see where this pattern begins and ends. The layering of colours and richness created gives an effect not unlike stained glass windows. Remember when you change to a crewel needle it is no longer necessary to count threads. This pattern can be used in any of its stages. It is used in the Needlework Accessories page 74 and up to Stage 3 in the Braithwaite Sampler.

STITCHES: Long tail chain, wrapping, fly and short tail chain.

USE: in blocks, bands or borders at any of its stages.

STAGE 1: Work the long tail chain stitches in a clockwise direction. Use a tapestry needle.

STAGE 2: Note the arrows on the diagram indicating the pairs to wrap. Start at the centre and wrap the long tails firmly in pairs. Wrap up toward the head of the chain stitch as shown, then take the needle down into the fabric to keep the wrapped chain straight and move onto the next pair.

STAGE 3: Change to a crewel needle. Without counting work a chain stitch in between the wrapping as shown (rust).

STAGE 4: Work a fly stitch in teal at the head of each chain stitch.

STAGE 5: Work a fly stitch in mustard at the other end of the rust chain stitch.

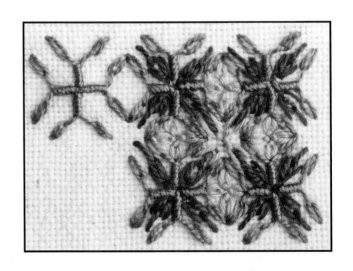

STAGE 6: Fly stitch filling - to give a glow vary the colours, sea green, purple.

STAGE 7: Work a straight stitch where indicated using pale green, it is couched within the fly stitch filling.

STAGE 8: Optional - use pale apricot and work fly stitch around the tails of some of the brick coloured chain stitches. It is used as a highlight only. Refer to the photograph for its placement.

OPTIONS: Long tail chain - the head can be worked over two, three or four threads and tail over four six, or eight threads respectively. Scale up the pattern for a cushion cover worked in wool on an 18-20 count linen.

Photograph: Blue option- Fabric: Belfast 32 count, Threads: DMC No 8 Perle 930, 992, three threads stranded 597, 3830, Anchor stranded 364, 568, 215, 216.
Shades of autumn option- Fabric: Lugana 25 count, Threads: No 8 Perle DMC 435,315, Anchor 0281, Coton a broder 16, 919, 471, 738.

Stitched as for Needlecase page 26

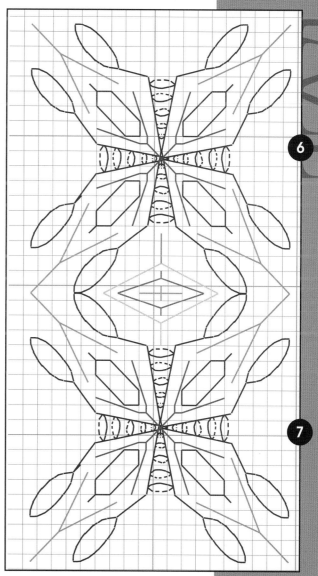

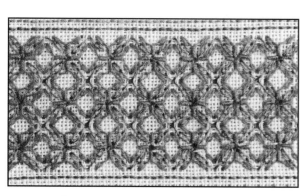

From Braithwaite Sampler page 79

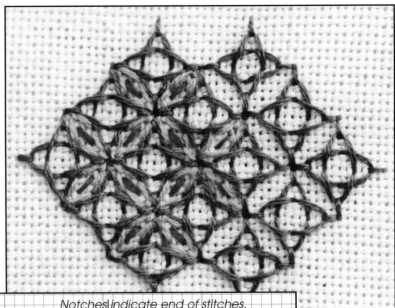

Notches indicate end of stitches.

WINCHESTER: from Melbourne Panel page 80.

Named for the magnificent Cathedral of Old Wessex. An adaptation of Lindisfarne II.

STITCHES: Fly, straight

USE: in blocks or bands.

OPTION: Further fillings could be selected; an ideal pattern worked in wool for a cushion cover

ORDER OF WORKING: Fly stitches blue (notches indicate end of each fly stitch), Change to a crewel needle Straight stitch green Fly stitch yellow

Photograph: Fabric: Lugana 25 count. Threads DMC No 8 Perle 930, 355, 833.

The following are a series of original stitch patterns that have evolved over the years of using and teaching this technique.

Aspiring Tussock: is named for the tall grasses that grow in our high country

STITCHES: Straight

USE: in bands borders or small units see Braithwaite Sampler page 79, space rows.

OPTION: Colour blend with two needles and threads using colours of similar value see page 19 for more information on colour blending.

Photograph: Fabric: 25 count Lugana. Threads: DMC No 8 Perle 315.

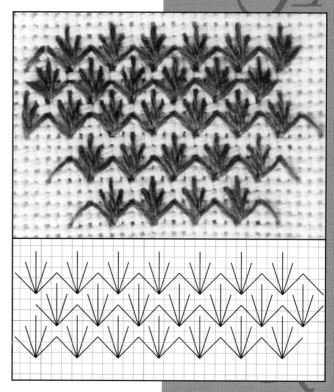

BRAITHWAITE

STITCHES: fly, wave and straight

USE: in bands and borders see Braithwaite Sampler page 79

OPTION: add extra stitches to fill the diamonds or change the lengths of the various stitches.

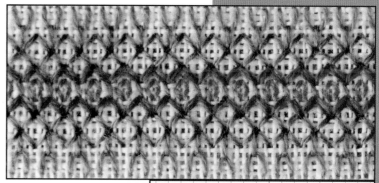

ORDER OF WORKING: Wave stitch blue, green (these I would work one diamond at a time), Straight stitch yellow, Fly orange

Photograph: Fabric Edinburgh 35 count linen. Threads DMC stranded one thread 931, 356, 355.

HANDY HINT: If a slight change of colour value would help to coordinate a design, select a very similar shade and stitch over one of the original lines of stitching. Shown in rust section of above photograph where one thread of 355 was worked over the top of 356 to give a slight shift in tone.

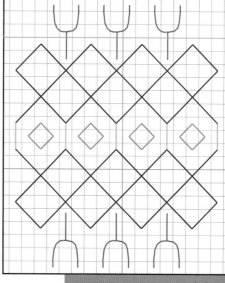

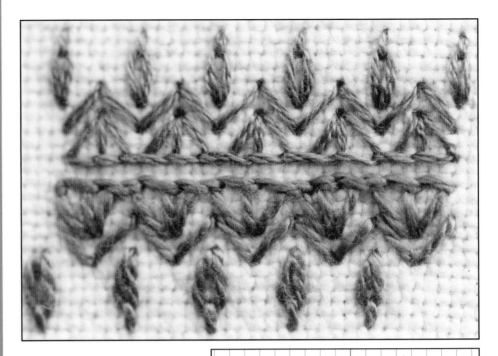

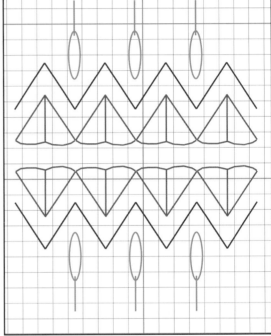

CARISBROOK

I drew this pattern while listening to a rugby match at Carisbrook, a local sports field. I thought that it looked like heads down and 'tails up' in a scrum. Note that for this pattern the buttonhole stitch is forming little pyramids, the first stitch slants to the right, the second is straight the third slants to the left.

STITCHES: buttonhole, wave and long tail chain

USE: as either a band or border see Abbie's Memory Pocket page 74

OPTION: enlarge or reduce the count to suit

ORDER OF WORKING: Buttonhole red, Wave blue, Chain orange.

Photograph: Fabric: Cotton 28 count, Threads: DMC No 8 Perle 3041.

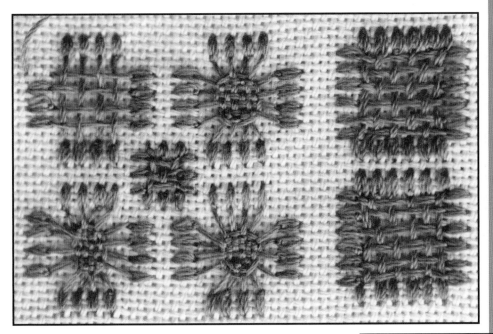

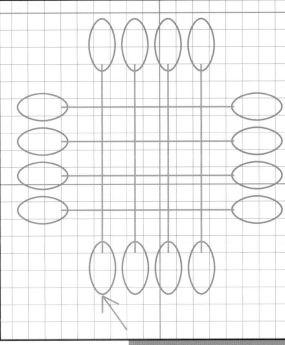

START HERE

DURHAM

Named because of Durham Cathedral's very close association with the Lindisfarne Gospels. Used on reverse side of Abbie's memory pocket. I wanted to incorporate interweaving which is a feature of Celtic art.

STITCH: A double headed long tail chain

USE: in blocks or bands.

OPTIONS: The head of the chain and the tail can both be varied in length to suit the area this stitch is to be worked in.

ORDER OF WORKING: When working each long tail chain, take the needle 2 - 3 threads under the fabric, turn and work a second head at the end of the long tail, see photograph with thread trailing ready to work second chain head.

Work the long tail chain grid first, darning the second side of the long tail chain stitches in and under the first side.

To pull the woven centre into a circular shape, darn over and under each long tail at the edge of the woven centre, taking the needle and thread around twice, pulling the centre into a circle.

Photograph: Fabric: Lugana 25 count. Threads: DMC stranded two threads of 320 and 931.

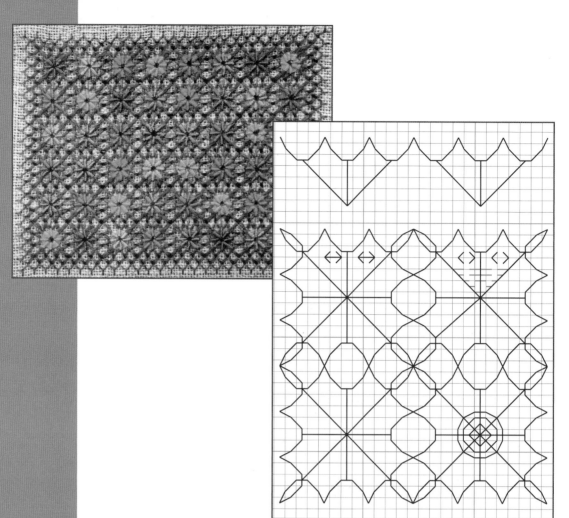

EXETER

This stitch pattern is named for the magnificent Exeter Cathedral of old Wessex.

STITCHES: Long tail fly

USE: in blocks bands or borders

OPTION: Work either back stitch spider's web or needle weaving around the tails.

ORDER OF WORKING: Long tail fly then back stitch spider's web or needle weaving. In back stitch spider's web the two long tails at each corner are treated as one. The needle weaving option pulls the three tails together on each side of the block - see arrows.

Photograph: Fabric 32 count Belfast Threads DMC stranded one thread each of 3832, 3837, 3835, 3838, 3850, 3851 3848, 3844, 3843, 3845 for the blue needlebook
One thread each of 3848 3847 3850, 3851, 3832 3833, 3853, 3854, 3852, 3835 for the green option.
One thread each of 3858, 3857, 3859, 3860, 3862, 3863, 3835, 3852 for the autumn toned option.

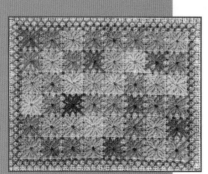

See Otago 150th year sampler page 75

STITCHES: wave and straight

USE: in bands borders

OPTION: change the scale by altering stitch length, work the straight stitches within the central diamonds, or try chain stitch, or further wave stitches to give a more solid effect.

ORDER OF WORKING: Wave stitch blue, red, Straight stitch green.

Photograph: Fabric: Glenshee Linen 28 count. Threads DMC stranded one thread 930 and 355.

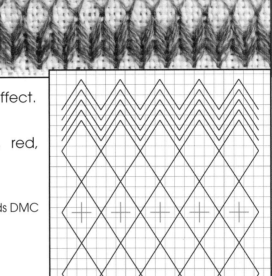

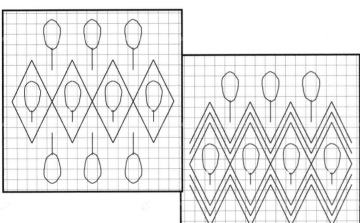

MANIOTOTO

Named for the mountains and Lombardy poplars which are a feature of that high country farming district in the South Island of New Zealand.

STITCHES: wave, long tail chain

USE: in blocks or bands add further stitches.

OPTION: Work wave stitch over more threads to increase the size of the pattern or stack further rows of wave stitch to add depth and density.

ORDER OF WORKING: Wave stitch blue, Long tail chain red.

Photograph: Fabric: Cotton 28 count. Threads: DMC stranded two threads 3722

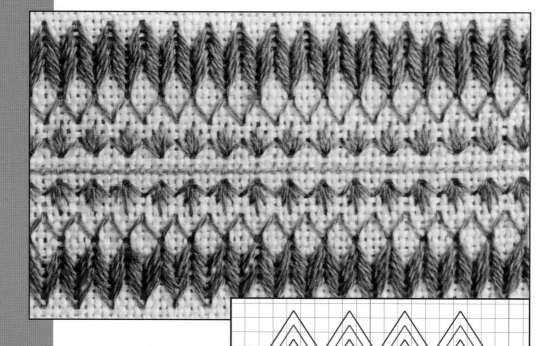

MORNINGTON

Mornington see Otago 150th Sampler page 75.

STITCHES: wave, straight, couching

USE: in bands

ORDER OF WORKING: Wave stitch blue, red, Straight stitch green, Couching orange

Photograph: Fabric Glenshee linen 28 count. Threads DMC stranded one thread of 931, 355, 833 and 3041.

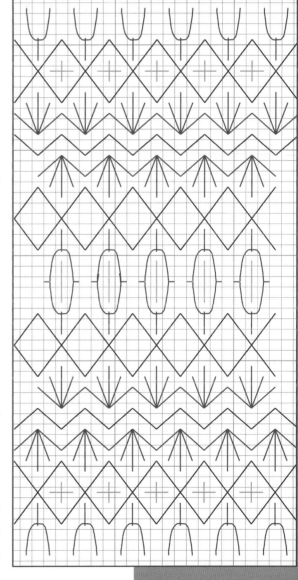

OTAGO

Named for its many mountains, rivers and rich farmland, see Braithwaite sampler page 79.

STITCHES: fly, wave, straight. Note the varying number of threads that the wave stitch is worked over.

USE: in bands

OPTION: change the order of different parts of the pattern to suit, work portions in the colour blending method.

ORDER OF WORKING: Fly stitch red (in central row of double fly stitches notch indicates end of each stitch), Wave stitch blue, Straight stitch green orange and pink, outer fly stitch red.

Photograph: Fabric: Edinburgh linen 35 count. Threads: Stranded cottons one thread of DMC 931, 356 and Anchor 320.

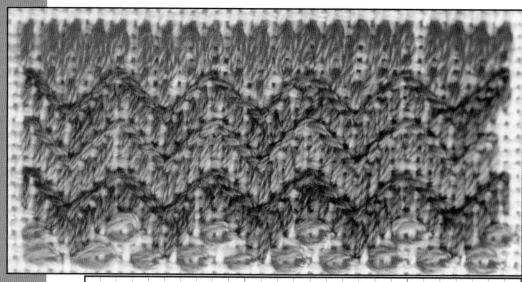

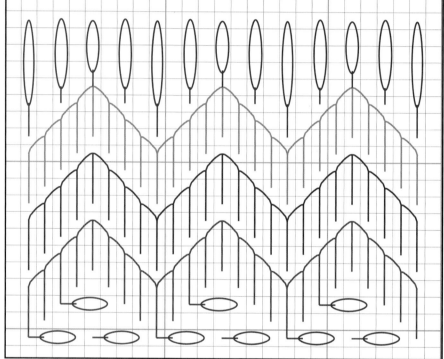

PACIFIC

Pacific is a stitch pattern inspired by the Tapa cloth, unique to the peoples of the many Pacific Islands, see Jaimee's memory pocket page 74.

STITCHES: buttonhole and detached chain

USE: in blocks or bands

OPTION: add further rows of the buttonhole, grade colour as for Florentine embroidery

ORDER OF WORKING: Buttonhole aqua, blue and green, Chain stitch red.

Photograph: Fabric: Lugana 25 count. Threads: stranded cottons two threads of DMC 501, 3768, 356, 3778 and Anchor 876.

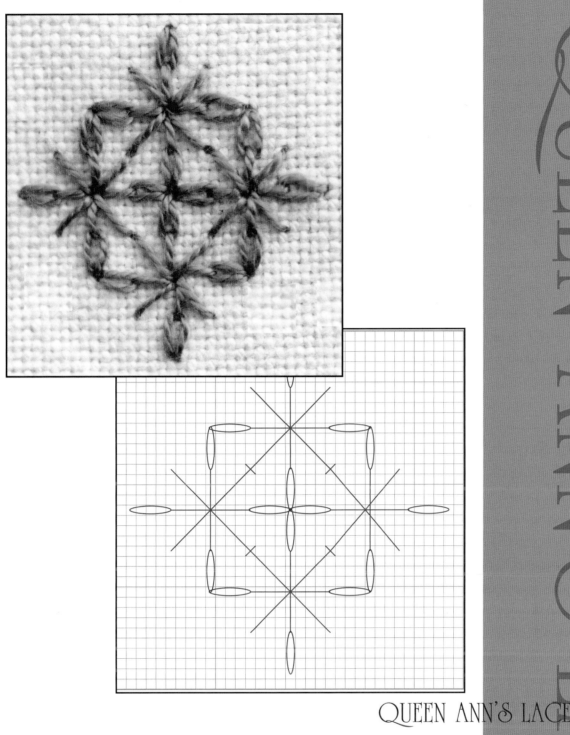

QUEEN ANN'S LACE

See the Taylor Memory Pocket page 74.

STITCHES: Long tail chain, straight

USE: in blocks, bands or borders.

OPTION: work half the pattern for a narrow band or border, Change the scale by working both the chain head and tail over two or three threads.

ORDER OF WORKING: Long tail chain red, Straight stitch green over four threads. Note notch indicates end of each stitch.

Photograph: Fabric: Cotton 28 count. Threads: DMC No 8 Perle cotton 992
Notches indicate end of stitches

SALISBURY

Named for the magnificent Wessex Cathedral see Jaimee's memory pocket page 74. An adaptation of Glastonbury.

STITCHES: wide fly, straight, chain. Note once the fly stitch grid is complete change to a sharp needle to fit the other stitches in. Use in blocks, bands, borders

OPTION: To fill the shape, work chain stitches, instead of straight or use the fly stitch grid only as a band or block. Increase the scale and work as an all over pattern in crewel wool on 18 - 20 count linens where it would be ideal for cushion covers.

ORDER OF WORKING: Wide fly stitch wine, straight stitch red, then change to a crewel needle for the following stitches, Fly green, Straight, yellow, blue.

Photograph: Fabric: Cotton 28 count. Threads: DMC stranded cottons, 355, 833, 931, 581. Initial fly stitch worked using two threads, balance of embroidery stitched using one thread.

Narrow borders are important. They are a useful method to fill spaces on samplers and to frame quotations. They give the opportunity to flow colour in varying proportions throughout the composition and unify each of the separate elements into a complete whole, see my samplers pages 75, 77 and 79.

Extensive use of narrow borders was made in these pieces, without them, the designs and colour would not have 'flowed' so well. Take time to trace with your finger the colour 'flow' through each sampler illustrated.

The narrow borders feature mainly back, straight, chain, couching and wave stitches and most of these borders are scaled down versions or sections of the stitch patterns. See the Dunstan

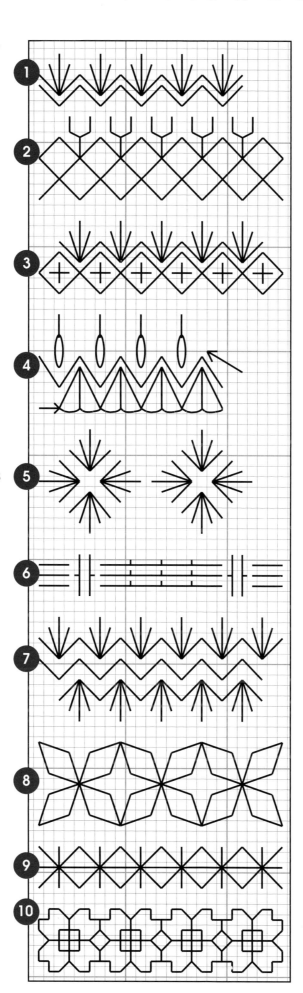

1. ASPIRING TUSSOCK - work just one row to complete a line of lettering or add a line of wave stitch to underline the tussock. See Braithwaite sampler

2. BRAITHWAITE: wave and fly stitch see Otago 150th and Braithwaite samplers

3. ROSLYN: wave and straight stitch, a useful border used in Otago and Braithwaite Samplers

4. CARISBROOK: - one half only, would border a quotation see Abbie's Memory Pocket

5. DUNEDIN: - as a row or isolated block - see Otago 150th sampler

6. FARM GATE: *back stitch From Mrs Foster's May 1918 sampler, see Otago 150th sampler

7. OTAGO: - any portion of this pattern is ideal as a narrow border and can be worked with at least two colours - see Braithwaite sampler

8. OUTRAM: - worked as one row only or try the scaled down version. Use one pattern to begin a sentence, see Otago 150th sampler

9. OVERCAST SQUARES: a very useful narrow border

10. PEMBROKE: one row of florets only, this pattern is ideal for the two or three needle and thread blending method

pattern, in the Millennium sampler page 77 where it has been scaled down and worked with the three needle and thread method. Many of the other narrow borders are also ideal for this method of 'flowing' colour through your composition.
This is not an exhaustive list of borders. Elements from virtually every stitch pattern could be used to create further borders.

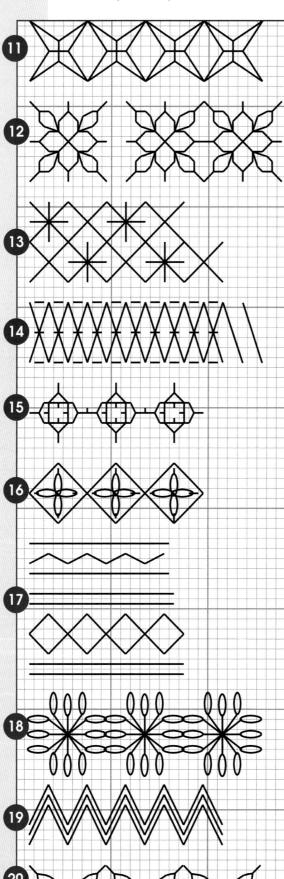

11. SALISBURY: an arrangement of fly stitch worked over four, six or eight threads

12. DUNSTAN: a scaled down version

13. NOUGHTS AND CROSSES: work one row as a border, or two as a frame for a quotation - ussed in this way on the hussifs

14. UNITED: stitch 5 'Embroidery '1934. scale up or down in height. Straight and back stitch

15. WINCHESTER: *fly stitch

16. LINDISFARNE I: Wave stitch diamonds, filled with either chain or straight stitches

17. WAVE AND BACKSTITCH: see Otago 150th and Braithwaite samplers

18. MRS FOSTER: - blocks of long tail chain worked in a row over a square of eight threads

19. IONA: - the stacked wave stitch portion, graduating colour with each row of wave stitch would be effective, see Otago 150th sampler

20. MERCURY ENERGY: - one row of the zig zag detached chain stitch

Notches indicate end of stitches

Refer to colour photograph page 74.

Greeting Cards, Spectacles Case, Handkerchief Sachet or Small Bags

There is something very special about an embroidered greeting. These 'memory pockets' can be designed to acknowledge special achievements, anniversaries, birthdays, or as a token of friendship. Embroidered greetings can be given as a card or made into a pocket or pouch to hold special items or mementos relating to the occasion. Abbie is going to keep jewellery in her birthday Memory Pocket. As another option, use the Memory Pocket as a Spectacles Case, a handkerchief sachet, or make it into a little bag with a drawstring around the top. The size of the Memory Pocket or Greeting Cards may be varied depending upon the overall design and their intended purpose.

I have stitched these using 32 count Belfast linen, remember the stitch designs are worked over more threads than other types of stitching so although the linen may be finer than you are used to, you are working on a larger scale than in many other types of counted thread embroidery.

MEMORY POCKET: 'Happy Birthday Abbie'

Finished size 15 x 9cm (6 x 3 1/2")
The stitch patterns I chose for this 'pocket' relate to different aspects of Abbie's life. A very special treat for Abbie is to go to Carisbrook with her father to watch the rugby, especially when the Otago team or the All Blacks are playing. Abbie also enjoys family trips in their four wheel drive over the high country Dunstan trail, from their home in Outram to the Maniototo. I chose the wonderful warm colours of the rhododendrons for Abbie's pocket because her families' nursery specialises in this beautiful shrub.

Requirements:

- Linen: 32 count Belfast 778, blue/grey 25 x 20 cm (10 x 8")
- Lining: Liberty or patchwork print or similar 26 x 21 cm (10 1/2 x 8 1/2")
- Threads: D.M.C Stranded cotton 309 deep pink; 401 orange, 603 bright pink; 3328 light terracotta; 3687 rose pink; 3803 raspberry.
- Use two threads of stranded cotton for the embroidery, one thread for the lettering and three threads for Antwerp buttonhole stitch.

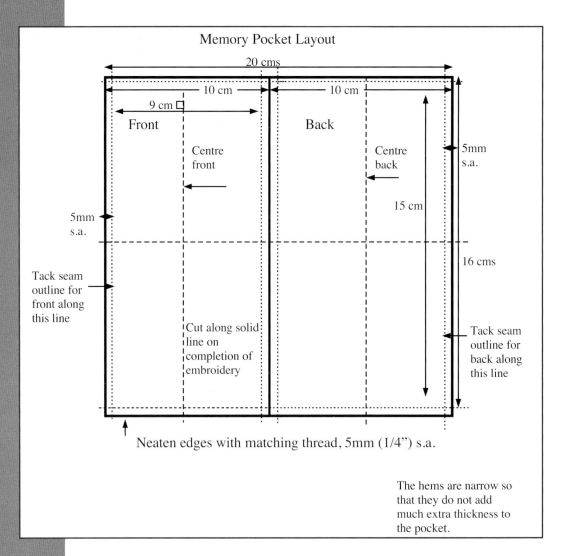

Memory Pocket Layout

20 cms

10 cm   10 cm

9 cm

Front   Back

Centre front   Centre back

5mm s.a.

15 cm

5mm s.a.

16 cms

Tack seam outline for front along this line

Cut along solid line on completion of embroidery

Tack seam outline for back along this line

Neaten edges with matching thread, 5mm (1/4") s.a.

The hems are narrow so that they do not add much extra thickness to the pocket.

Stitch patterns:

'Dunstan Trail' page 37, 'Carisbrook page 56' reverse side 'Durham' page 57

To Prepare Linen

Machine neaten the outer edge of the linen, see before you begin page 14. Refer to the layout diagram and tack where indicated, to mark the seam allowances and the centre back and front as a guide for placement of your embroidery. Cut the two pieces of linen apart, only after the embroidery has been completed.

To stitch the pattern

Measure 2.5 cm (1") down and 1.5 cm (1/2") in from the tacked seam line at the top left hand corner and start working Dunstan trail see page 37. It is worked over 12 x 12 threads.
Carisbrook is placed with the base of the pattern 2.5 cm up and 1.5 cm in from the tacked seam line at the lower right hand corner. See page 22 for placement of text.

I worked five repeats of the stitch pattern Durham on the reverse of the Abbie's memory pocket. Four were worked over 16 threads, four threads apart and a very small version was worked in the centre with name and date beneath. The patterns were placed starting at the centre and working down.

To Construct the Memory Pocket

1. On the completion of all embroidery, cut the two pieces of linen apart and machine neaten the raw edges within the 5mm seam allowance.

2. Fold down the corners to mitre them, pin to hold in place, fold down the seam allowance and tack seam and corners in place.

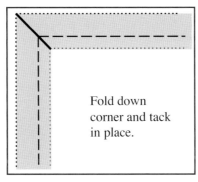

Fold down corner and tack in place.

3. Pin both the linen and lining wrong sides together through the centre lengthwise on the straight grain of the lining and along the central tacked line on the linen. The lining is a little larger than the linen as it is not as easy to cut accurately as the linen and this does make it easier to handle. Fold in the edges of the lining to the exact size of the linen, pin then tack to hold. (It is not necessary to mitre the corners of the lining.)

4. Join the linen and lining together by working Antwerp knotted buttonhole stitch (see page 25) over three linen threads, three threads apart and through both fabrics. Use a crewel needle and either three threads of stranded cotton or No 8 Perle. Stitch evenly and make sure new thread joins do not show. To bring in a new thread invisibly see page 15.

5. To join the back and front of the memory pocket together work a second row of Antwerp buttonhole stitch into the loops in the first row of stitching worked on both pieces being joined.

HANDY HINT: By making the lining a little larger than the linen it 'spreads' the thickness of the seam allowance.

MEMORY POCKET: 'Congratulations Jaimee'

Finished size 15cm x 9cm(6 x 3 1/2")

Refer to colour photograph page 74

Jaimee and her family spend summer holidays on their yacht sailing in the beautiful Hauraki Gulf. I designed the Pacific pattern to reflect this family activity. My inspiration came from the Tapa cloth patterns of the people of the Pacific region. The colours are those of the Pacific Ocean at dawn. Jaimee's father is a minister and the Salisbury and Lindisfarne II patterns reflect something of the families involvement in the church.

Requirements:

- Linen: 32 count Belfast 778, blue/grey 25 x 20 cm (10 x 8") or size to suit your project
- Lining: Liberty or patchwork print or similar 26 x 21 cm (10 1/2 x 8 1/2")
- Threads as listed:

Stranded cotton DMC: 817 scarlet, 921 orange, 3765 teal, 3807 blue/violet*, 924 slate grey*. One thread was used for the embroidery and lettering, three threads were used for Antwerp buttonhole stitch.

*indicates DMC threads colours substituted for Anchor colours, 122, 9378.

Stitch patterns:

'Salisbury' page 64, 'Pacific' page 62 reverse side 'Lindisfarne II' page 40

To stitch the pattern

Refer to 'Congratulations Abbie' for 'To Prepare Linen' page 68.

Measure 2.5 cm (1") down and 1.5 cm (1/2") in from the tacked seam line at the top left hand corner and start working Salisbury. Pacific is started 4 cm (1 1/2") up from the lower tacked seam line and 1.5 cm in from the left hand side tacked seam line. See page 22 for placement of text. Back stitch in orange is worked under all text and wave stitch in purple is worked under third row of text and in teal under the final row of text. This flows the colour through the composition.

One pattern of Lindisfarne II has been centred on the back of the 'pocket' with my name and date beneath it.

Make up the pocket following To Construct the Memory Pocket page 69.

MEMORY POCKET: Taylor family's New Baby

Finished size 15cm x 9cm(6 x 3 1/2")

Refer to colour photograph page 74

The Taylor family live in Cromwell, the heart of the pip and stone fruit and the local wine industry region of Otago. During the Otago gold rush of the 1860's Cromwell was an important town and early miners and pioneers planted thyme as well as many other plants to enhance their surroundings. During spring and early summer the hills, valleys and roadways are aglow with the mauves and lavenders of this beautiful fragrant herb. The colours of this pocket reflect the colours of Cromwell, the patterns something of the town's special features - including thyme which has a mass of florets as does Queen Ann's Lace. Many of the fruit trees and grapevines are espaliered and look similar to the 'pineapple' with its 'fence like' supports.

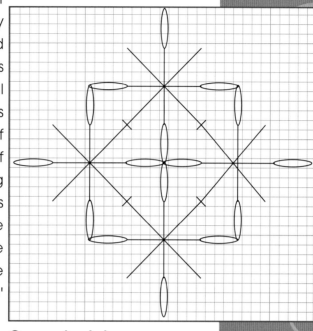

Queen Ann's Lace

Requirements:

- Linen: 32 count Belfast 778, blue/grey 25 x 20 cm (10 x 8") or size to suit your project
- Lining: Liberty or patchwork print or similar 26 x 21 cm (10 1/2 x 8 1/2")
- Threads as listed:

Stranded cotton D.M.C: 3834 deep violet, 3835 violet, 581 yellow green, 561 blue/green.

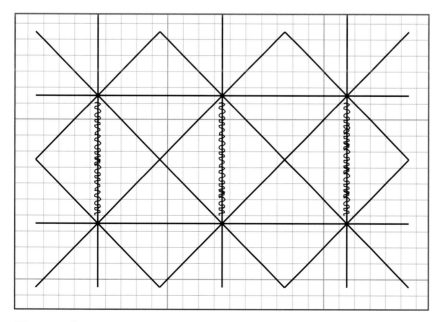

Pineapple

Stitch patterns:

' Queen Ann's Lace' page 63 'Pineapple' page 49 reverse side 'Mountain Beech' page 43

To stitch the pattern

Refer to 'Congratulations Abbie' for 'To prepare linen' page 68. There was quite a lot of text I wished to include on this memory pocket so its placement was worked out first on paper. A narrow pattern of Queen Anne's Lace was stitched beneath the first text block and the Pineapple stitch pattern was stitched beneath the second text block.

When stitching 'Queen Anne's Lace' I used two threads of stranded cotton. For the violet portion of the pattern I worked with three shades of violet in the three needles and threads blending colour see page 19. To give the third shade of violet, one of the three needles was threaded with one strand each of deep violet and violet. When working the 'Pineapple' stitch pattern, work with two threads of stranded cotton except for the needle weaving where one thread is used. To highlight the text underneath it I worked two rows of back stitch in violet and yellow green.

On the reverse four pattern repeats of Mountain Beech were stitched, starting at the centred and working down, using one thread of violet. I stitched my name and the date beneath the patterns. One thread of stranded cotton was used for the lettering, three threads were used for Antwerp buttonhole stitch.

Make up the pocket following 'To Construct the Memory Pocket' page 69.

HANDY HINT: make a card or book mark using these patterns for a charming and quickly made gift.

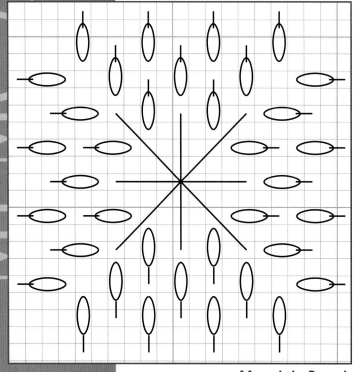

Mountain Beech

MEMORY POCKETS

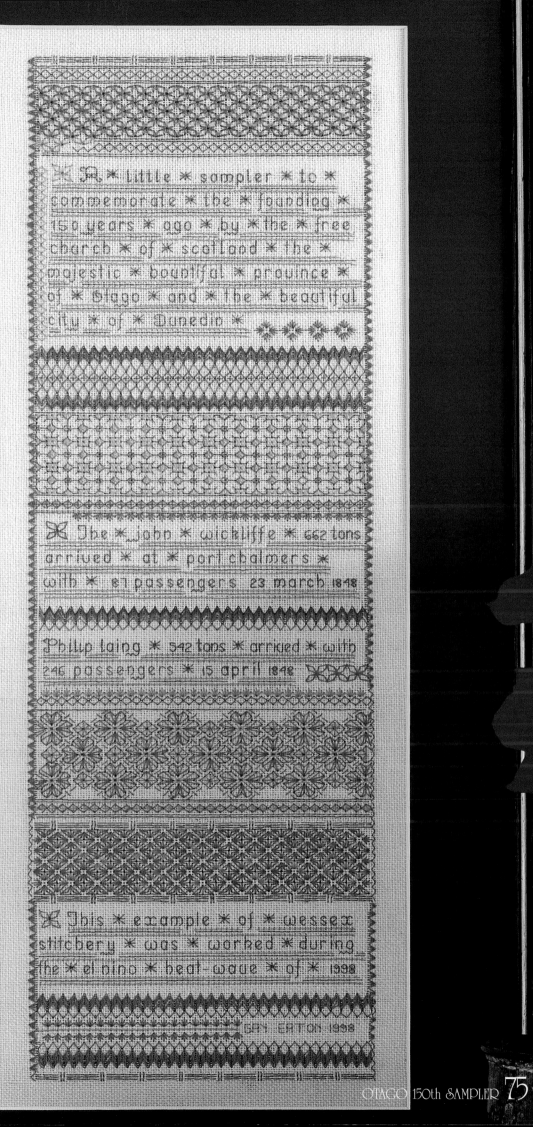

A * little * sampler * to * commemorate * the * founding * 150 years * ago * by * the * free church * of * scotland * the * majestic * bountiful * province * of * Otago * and * the * beautiful city * of * Dunedin *

The * john * wickliffe * 662 tons arrived * at * port chalmers * with * 97 passengers 23 march 1848

Philip laing * 542 tons * arrived * with 246 passengers * 15 april 1848

This * example * of * wessex stitchery * was * worked * during the * el nino * heat-wave * of * 1998

GEN ERTON 1998

TRAY CLOTH

...eneath the rule of men entirely great, the pen is mightier than the sword. Bulwer-Lytton 1803-1873

The printing press was the invention of the second millennium A.D. that has brought the most benefit to mankind. From Johann Gutenberg's invention in 1440 sprang an industry with extraordinary rapidity, wherever the craving for literacy, knowledge wisdom, truth, freedom and communication was demanded

My prayer for the third millenniun is: Let the pen be mightier than the sword so that the lion will lay down with the lamb.

This little sampler was completed as Dunedin's 120 year old town hall clock's midnight chimes rang in the dawn of the new millennium around the world via television one New Zealand. and the B.B.C.

By 1274 the Braithwaite Family were well established at York. This little sampler records our direct line from Thomas of Beilby 1577-1616 yeoman farmer of Hayton-cum-beilby, east riding of Yorkshire m. Margaret _ * ralph * elizabeth * jane * alice *** Ralph 1605-1665 m. Elizabeth Hutchenson * james * thomas * ann * elizabeth * marmaduke *** Thomas 1635-1689 m. Elizabeth Sandes * john * thomas * elizabeth ***

Thomas 1675-1727 m. Ann Ward * john * elizabeth *** John 1704-1784 m. Mary Beilby * anne * john *** John 1761-1833 m. Elizabeth Preston * mary * anne * elizabeth * ellen * john * sarah * william * jane * robert * margaret ***

In 1820 the effects of the Land Enclosures had reached East Riding * Farmers had to find other means of livelihood for their sons * John 1795-1858 a tailor left the farmstead and moved to Holmfirth West Riding * m. Mary Cartwright * elizabeth * william * henry * george * mary * ann * martha *

William 1821-1891 m. Hannah Armitage * john * ammon * martha * fred * harry * willie * emma * mary *** Harry 1859-1928 m. Mary Hannah Charlesworth * arthur * herbert * harold *** Harold 1891-1958 m. Harriet Ann Lee * dorothy j *** Dorothy J. 1923 m. Brian Lodge * david * philip ***

Our Braithwaites are of anglo-saxon origin * the name means broad field *** Research * Dorothy J. Lodge * Holmfirth

GAI EATON N.Z. 1995

**Reverse of
Melbourne Panel**

Melbourne Panel

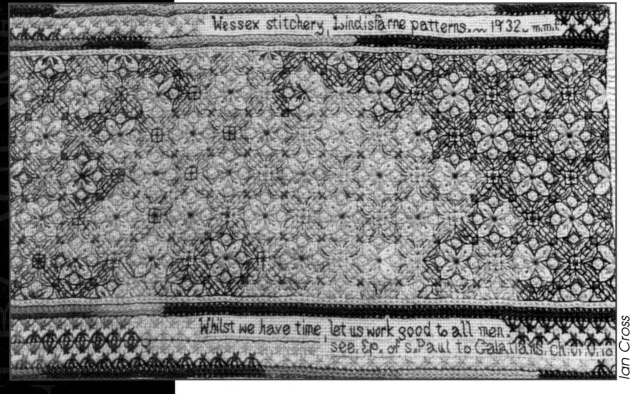

Wessex stitchery, Lindisfarne patterns. ~ 1932. m.m.f.

Whilst we have time, let us work good to all men.
see. Ep. of s.Paul to Galatians ch.vi.v.10

Ian Cross

Gay Eaton

Cushion Stitched by Rachel Dunbar

Stitch Patterns: Nigellia and Exeter
Threads: One strand Appleton wool using the two or three
needle and thread method.
Linen: Cork

THE BUTTERCUP MEADOW HUSSIF & POPPY PATCH HUSSIFS

Finished size 25 x 9 cm (10 x 3 1/2")

See colour photograph page 78.

'Hussif' also spelt 'huswif' is an abbreviation of 'housewife' described in the Dictionary of Fashion and Costume as *a small container with set of sewing essentials such as needles, thread, scissors, thimble, etc.* They have been popular for centuries, shapes vary and the techniques used to decorate them change with the fashion but the basic hussif as a holder of essential sewing equipment is always useful and popular. The hussifs* featured here are extremely practical 'containers' of sewing essentials with a little needlebook at one end, and a drawstring at the other, to close the pouch containing the sewing equipment. The drawstring is no ordinary cord - it is a hand made finger cord with hand made toggles attached and full instructions are given for these. The 'Buttercup Meadow' and 'Poppy Patch' hussifs combine beauty with practicality and would make a most attractive personalised gift for a travelling or sewing friend or a grandchild. Both are made in the same way, by changing the colours of the 'flowers', they could become a rose garden, perennial border, or a lovely patch of wild flowers!

*The design for this hussif first came to New Zealand in a 'Loan Packet' from the London Embroiderers' Guild when it was decorated with Blackwork. Threads 8/84 April 1984.

PLEASE NOTE: Should you choose to work a different Stitch Pattern, or use a different linen allow extra fabric and remember to include seam allowances. Begin the embroidery at the tacked centre of the main piece, complete all the stitch pattern blocks to establish the finished size before tacking hemlines and the reverse side. For information on alternative linens and the threads to use with them refer to page 11.

Requirements

- Linen: Zweigart 32 count Belfast linen in a deep green colour (641) 30 x 30 cm (12 x 12") to give two pieces 11 x 26cm (4 1/4 x 10 1/2") for the hussif, two pieces 3 cm sq (1 1/4"sq) for the scissors tag and two pieces 3.5 x 8cm (1 1/2 x 3 1/4") for the toggles. The Margaret stitch pattern is worked over twenty four threads. Remember although the linen may be finer than you are used to, you are working on a larger scale than in many other types of stitching.

- Lining: Two pieces 13 x 28cm (5 1/4 x 11") cotton print fabric to match
- Finger Cord is required for the drawstrings and to attach the scissors to the scissors tag. It is made using No 8 Perle cotton or stranded cotton and full instructions for making it are on page 103. (Total length approx. 1.5 m or 1 1/2 yds.)
- Flannel for the needle book pages 10 x 13cm (3 1/2 x 4 3/4") - a larger piece is easier to work with.
- Ecru Perle 8 for stitching the edges of the needlebook pages
- Threads as listed:
  Greens, same colours used in both hussifs - DMC No 8 Perle or stranded cottons 320, 367, 469, 580, 3345, 3346,
The Buttercup Hussif
Buttercups - DMC No. 8 Perle 726, 743, 727*, 973*
Threads: The Poppy Hussif
Poppies - 309, 321, 498, 600, 3687*, 817
Finishing: No 8 Perle or three threads of stranded cotton (DMC 501).
Alternatively use a selection of threads from your collection remembering that three threads of stranded cotton equal one thread of Perle 8.
*indicates DMC threads colours substituted for Anchor colours 293, Semco 193, Anchor 77, which were used in the embroidery.

Stitch pattern:

Front - 'Margaret' page 84, Back - 'Noughts and Crosses' page 46. The Margaret stitch pattern is worked over twenty four threads. The central stitch 'head' is worked over three with the tail worked over nine threads and the stitches on either side have the tail worked over six threads. (NB The pattern given on page 41 is worked over 16 threads.) 'Noughts and Crosses' is stitched as shown.

To Begin

Machine neaten the fabric (see to neaten edges page 14). Refer to the layout guide for placement of the hussif, tag and toggles on the linen page 86. Refer to the Hussif layout guide and tacking over and under four threads at all times, tack the outlines of the back and front of the hussif, the seam allowances, the centre front and back, the cord and needle case lines. Note that the horizontal centre line is 10 cm (4") below the cord casing line, this ensures that the pattern is displayed nicely when the pouch is closed and not hidden in the gathers. Tack the outline of the scissors tag and toggles also. Do not cut out the fabric pieces until all embroidery is completed. There is a 5 mm (1/4") seam allowance on all raw edges.

Hussif Layout

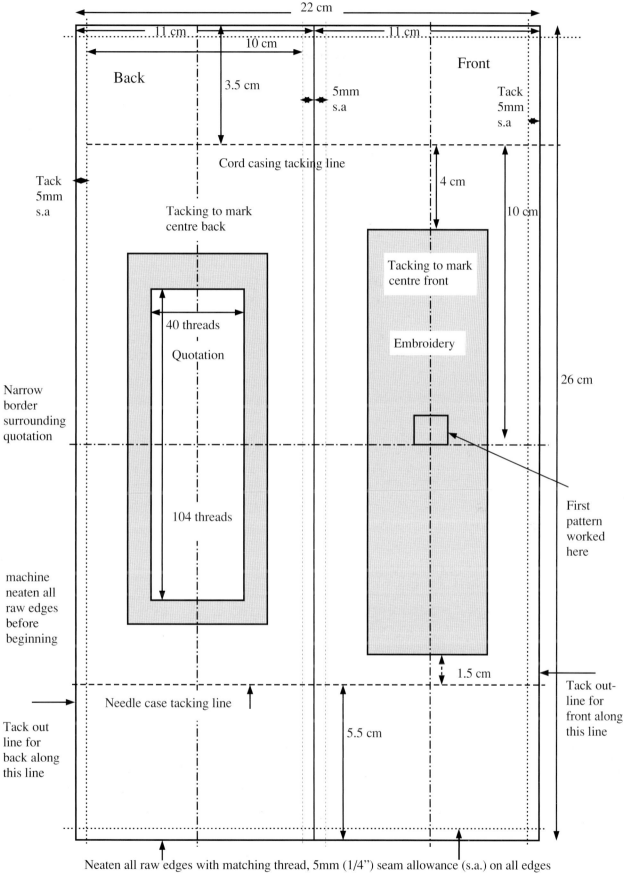

22 cm

11 cm · 11 cm

10 cm

Back

Front

3.5 cm

5mm s.a

Tack 5mm s.a

Cord casing tacking line

Tack 5mm s.a

4 cm

10 cm

Tacking to mark centre back

Tacking to mark centre front

Embroidery

40 threads

Quotation

Narrow border surrounding quotation

26 cm

First pattern worked here

104 threads

machine neaten all raw edges before beginning

1.5 cm

Tack out line for back along this line

Needle case tacking line

Tack out line for front along this line

5.5 cm

Neaten all raw edges with matching thread, 5mm (1/4") seam allowance (s.a.) on all edges

NB The horizontal centre tacking line is 10 cm below the Cord Casing tacking line

Cut out on solid lines on completion of all embroidery

HUSSIF

The Margaret Stitch Pattern with the needle weaving option was selected for the front of the two hussifs as it lends itself to the floral effect I was wishing to create. Begin at the tacked centre and work the central long tail chain stitch with the 'head' of the chain stitch over three threads and the tail over nine. The shorter stitches on either side are worked with the head of the chain over three threads and the tail over six threads.

To give the effect of foliage I used a variety of green threads selected at random. To create the buttercups or poppies needle weave over each group of three chain stitches using a variety of yellow or red threads. Every stitch pattern does not have needle weaving, refer to the photograph for additional detail.

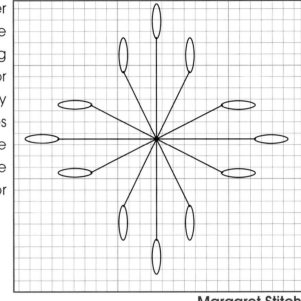

Margaret Stitch

Work the Noughts and Crosses pattern (page 46) to frame the Quotation *Stitching -is a -gentle -art to --ease the -soul -and -soothe -the -heart,* source unknown, on the reverse of the Buttercup Hussif and *To tell -a -woman what she -may not -do -is to -tell her -what she -can.* (Portuguese Proverb, Oxford book of Quotations) on the reverse of the Poppy Hussif.

See to Place Pattern as a Frame page 21 and Placement of Text page 22.

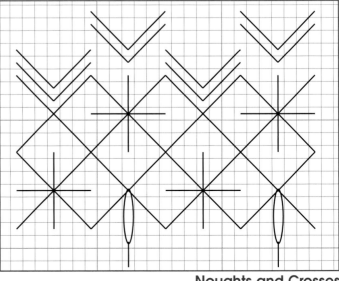

Noughts and Crosses

The overcast squares were stitched in shades of red (Poppy Hussif) or yellow (Buttercup Hussif) with all other stitching in shades of green. The green was stitched using Perle 8 thread in two different shades and the red and yellow overcast squares were stitched using two threads of stranded cottons. Select the different greens, yellows and reds in a random fashion. Fly stitches and detached chains were worked around the patterns edge to give a 'garden border' look.

Using the colour of your choice stitch the text using one thread of stranded cotton in Mrs Foster's style of lettering see page 22 .

Making The Flannel Pages

Cut the flannel 2 cm (3/4") larger than the required finished size of 9 x 10 cm (3 1/2 x 4"). To mark the finished size withdraw one thread on each side. It will also give a channel to work into and a cutting guide when the stitching is complete. With matching No 8 Perle thread, work buttonhole stitches between each thread and over three or four fabric threads, right round the edge of the 'page'. Because both sides of the 'page' are seen, start and finish threads by darning them into the weave of the flannel at the corners (which strengthens them) and cover with stitching. When the stitching is complete carefully clip the extra fabric away from beside the stitching. This method of working ensures nice flat 'pages' without wavy edges!

The Scissors Tag finished size 2 cm sq (3/4"sq)

Work one 'Margaret' stitch pattern in the centre of each tacked square. Embroider the needle weaving in the appropriate colour. Tack the seam line four threads beyond the pattern.

Finger Cord

Full instructions for making finger cord are given on page 103. Finger cords are used to close the pouch and to attach the tag to the scissors. Three lengths of cord are required. Two equal lengths of 45 cm (18") are required for the drawstring, a third length of 30 cm (12") is for the scissors. Cut the thread for your cord five times the finished length required, i.e. 225 cm (90") and 150 cm (60"). Make finger cord the required length and leave the extra thread trailing to be used to attach the cord to the toggles and to work detached buttonhole to cover the ends of the toggles. The extra cord for the scissor tag is used to buttonhole the two pieces together.

The drawstrings are threaded through the cord casing channel with a large tapestry needle or bodkin, they enter, turn, then exit from the side they entered so that there is a cord for each side of the pouch to pull to close it. The toggles are attached after the cord is threaded through the channel.

Layout of pieces for Hussif, Scissors fob and toggles
Linen 30 cm sq or 12" sq.

Scissors fob
3 x 6 cm (1/14 x 2 1/2")
includes s.a. of 5 mm

Toggles
2 pieces 3.5 x 8cm
(1 1/2 x 3") includes
s.a. of 5 mm

Hussif
22 cm x 26 cm (8 1/2 x 10 1/2")
includes s.a. of 5 mm

The Toggles

Finished size 2 cm in length 1 cm diam. (3/4" length 1/2" diam)
Full instructions for making these are given on page 106.
At the end of each toggle work Back Stitch spider's web in the appropriate colour (see page 24).

To construct the hussif

1. On the completion of all embroidery, cut the two pieces of linen apart and machine neaten the raw edges in the 5mm seam allowance, see before you begin page 14.

2. Fold down the corners to mitre, pin to hold in place, fold down the seam allowance and tack the seam allowances and corners in place.

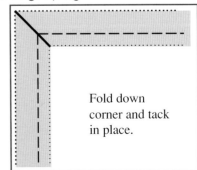

Fold down
corner and tack
in place.

3. Pin both the linen and lining wrong sides together through the centre lengthwise on the straight grain of the lining and along the central tacked line on the linen. The lining is a little larger than the linen as it is not as easy to cut accurately as the linen and this does make it easier to handle. Fold in the edges of the lining to the exact size of the linen, pin then tack to hold. (It is not necessary to mitre the corners of the lining.)

4. Next make the cord channel. Work a row of double running stitch, through both the linen and lining, along the tacked cord casing line. Take care to keep the stitching straight by checking from side to side as you stitch. Work a second row 1 cm (1/2") above the first. Stitch using three threads of stranded cotton or Perle 8.

5. Join the linen and lining together by working Antwerp knotted buttonhole stitch (see page 25) over three linen threads, three threads apart and through both fabrics. Do not sew the cord channel together. Use a crewel needle and either three threads of stranded cotton (DMC 501) or No 8 Perle. Stitch evenly. See page 15 for how to bring in a new thread invisibly.

6. Do this for both the front and back.

7. To join the back and front of the hussif together: Using three threads of stranded cotton or Perle 8 work a second row of Antwerp buttonhole stitch into the loops of the first row of Antwerp buttonhole stitch on both pieces of fabric being joined. Stitch between the lower edge of the cord channel and tacked needle case line only.

8. Fold the flannel page, pin or tack firmly in place with a little of the fold beyond the tacked line. Work double running stitch accurately along the tacked line, taking care to stitch through all layers. (Check from side to side as you stitch to ensure you are stitching on the tacked line.)

9. Embroider your name and date inside the needle case flap. Use the Tea bag method see page 109.

HANDY HINT: Finger pressing is very useful in embroidery as you have more control over your fingers than an iron.

To Make the Scissors tag

1. Mitre the corners and fold the seam allowance down along the tacked lines on both pieces of fabric, tack in place. Use the threads left at the beginning of the finger cord to attach the doubled length of finger cord to the wrong side of one piece of the tag at the corner. Use the threads left at the end of the finger cord (three threads at a time or one thread of Perle 8) to join the two pieces of the tag together by working buttonhole stitch over two threads and between each thread right round the tag.

2. Attach the tag to your scissors then place the scissors inside the hussif and thread the tag under the drawstring cord so that the tag is outside the hussif. This makes your scissors easy to find every time!

You will find this hussif an extremely useful needlework accessory - everything you need is in one place. Small and neat, it is easy to pick up and pop in your handbag to take with you where ever you are going, be it a stitch evening with friends or waiting for your children.

HANDY HINT: Fine stem stitch gives a good line that flows well for a signature

Wessex Stitchery is an ideal technique for decorative samplers that document special events and information of interest: family occasions such as births, marriage, memorials, unique civic events, historical records, academic and sporting achievements. It is also an excellent way to record genealogy and list family lines.

It was Mrs Foster's May 1918 sampler that sparked my initial interest in this technique. The little verse stitched there talked of a day of prayer for peace in 1918 that is possibly not recorded anywhere else (see page 8). For this reason I always try to include in my Samplers short comments of local interest and trust that these inclusions will make my work of more interest and value to future generations. It is a characteristic of Wessex Stitchery which I hope you too will want to continue.

Choosing Colours

When selecting colours for the samplers, choose no more than five or six. Of that number, select two to three that are the same value, include the main colour in this group. One of this group should be a little darker or lower in value. Limiting the number of colours and shades to work with, will help you to use each colour well. It is important that each colour travels, in varying proportions, harmoniously through the composition, some taking a more dominant role than others. In the Otago 150th Sampler blue is the dominant colour, it blends well with the green of the same value, the gold acts as a highlight and the violet (antique lilac) is much less dominant, yet is used for accents and can be found in varying proportions throughout the sampler. Rose and brick have been used sparingly as a strong contrast. Narrow borders are a useful way to carry colour harmoniously through a composition.

Separate the selected colours from the rest of your threads. Remember the threads can vary in weight and texture depending upon your design. For example in the Millennium Sampler I used stranded cottons and Perle 8. For the two fine samplers (Otago and Braithwaite) I used one thread of stranded cotton but you could also include DMC flower or silk threads.

The linen, threads, colours and stitch patterns used to embroider each of the samplers are listed. Whilst the text is only of limited relevance, it is given as a guide for planning your own. Colours and patterns are likewise given as a guide. This technique works well on different weights of linen so remember to choose a linen that you find comfortable to work with. Refer to page 12 for the threads to use on the different linens.

To plan a sampler

The Braithwaite and Otago 150th are Band Samplers.

When planning your Sampler consider text as a band of pattern and aim to work the text and stitch patterns in unequal sized bands. Work one or two bands of lettering first leaving space for the bands of pattern, then begin the stitch patterns so that you can visualise how your sampler will look. Continue working the sampler in this manner.

The placement of text for a band sampler is different to the placement of text within a frame of stitch pattern as seen on the Hussifs, Memory Pockets, Needlecase etc.

Decide the information that you want to record and prepare the text on paper or on your computer in uneven sized paragraphs with reference to the notes given on text placement page 22. Do not graph out. Stitch the text as you would handwriting, adjusting the space between letters and words to suit the space.

- Tack the left hand margin.
- The first row of text is worked before any pattern but leaving space for a band of pattern above the text. Work one row of text to establish the width of the sampler.
- Tack the right hand margin. If the line of text is too long, the band of text may not be deep enough.
- Work bands of text, leaving space for stitch patterns, each to be of a different depth.

The wealth of narrow borders allows freedom of colour placement as well as extending stitch patterns. They will fill any spaces between the bands of text and stitch patterns and give the opportunity to 'flow' colour throughout the composition.

HANDY HINT: if you wish to make the text area wider after you have finished stitching the text add a narrow vertical border.

To aid my pattern making rows of back stitch and couching were stitched under the words breaking the line at intervals to accommodate either capitals or the tails of letters, see Samplers pages 75 and 79. If a line of lettering has not finished in a pleasing place, Narrow Borders are a useful method to complete the space. Adhering to Mrs Foster's philosophy I do not graph out either the text or bands of stitch patterns.

There are a number of ways of spacing text. For the Otago 150th Sampler each word was separated with an overcast square. Individual motifs from many of the stitch patterns work well as markers for the start of each block of text or to fill in the spaces at the end of rows. Narrow border patterns can also be used to 'fill in'. If you wish to include a lot of text you may choose to use a finer linen to accommodate it, e.g. Edinburgh 35 count. Alternatively a smaller alphabet could be used on a linen with a lower thread count with letters and words worked closer together.

A GENEALOGICAL SAMPLER - The Braithwaite Sampler

See colour photograph page 79

Genealogy is a subject that interests many. In my case a lot of research on our family tree had been done by my cousin and I wanted to display this information in an accessible and easily understood manner. Wessex Stitchery was the perfect medium.

With all the information gathered the challenge was to decide what to include and what to leave out. I chose to include only my direct line from Thomas of Beilby one of three brothers of the Braithwaite family who farmed at Hayton-cum-Beilby, approx 23 miles from York. To give a personal angle to my family tree, I chose to include the reason for the family leaving their farm and moving to Holmfirth and the meaning of the family name. It was stitched in colours I like and to suit the furnishings of my cousin's home (this sampler's eventual home). 'Pastoral' type patterns were chosen to suit our farming background.

Requirements

- Linen: Edinburgh 35 count colour antique white 40 x 80 cm (16 x 32). Allow generously for the length of the Sampler. Wessex Stitchery can be worked on different linen counts see page 11 for recommended alternative linens.
- Threads as listed:
DMC stranded cottons: blue 931, blue green 3816*, green 320, rose 3722, antique lilac 3041, gold 833, extra colours used in colour blending brick 356, dusky rose 315. One thread of stranded cotton was used throughout. *indicates DMC thread colour substituted for Anchor 876 used in the embroidery.

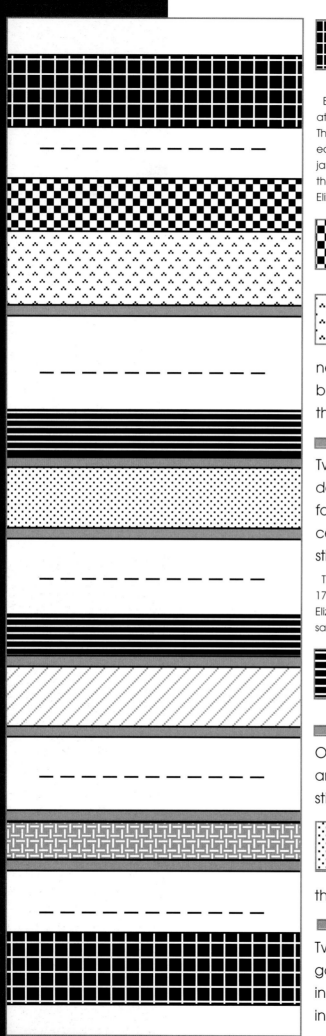

 ### OTAGO, VARIATION
minus the central fly stitches
Threads: blue, gold, blue/green

By 1274 the Braithwaite Family were well established
at York. This little sampler records our direct line from
Thomas of Beilby 1577-1616 yeoman farmer of Hayton-cum-beilby,
east riding of Yorkshire m. Margaret ralph elizabeth
jane alice *** Ralph 1605-1665 m Elizabeth Hutchenson, james
thomas ann elizabeth marmaduke ***Thomas 1635 -1689 m
Elizabeth Sandes john thomas elizabeth ***

 ### BRAITHWAITE
Threads: blue fly and outer wave stitch
Brick and rose for central rows

 ### PEMBROKE
Threads: brick, rose and dusky rose
were worked together, in the three
needle and thread technique see page 19. The
brick and rose shades are of similar value whilst
the dusky rose adds depth.

 ### NARROW BORDER
Two rows of back stitch in brick and antique lilac,
double row of wave stitch in green worked to
form a diamond with an upright cross in the
centre worked in gold, three more rows of back
stitch, two antique lilac and one gold.

Thomas 1675-1727 m Ann Ward john elizabeth *** John
1724-1784 m Mary Beilby anne john *** John 1761-1833 m
Elizabeth Preston mary anne elizabeth ellen john
sarah william jane robert margaret***

 ### ASPIRING TUSSOCK - THREE ROWS
Threads: blue and blue/green using the
two thread and needle method.

 ### NARROW BORDER
One row of wave stitch worked in
antique lilac with a row of gold back
stitching on either side.

 ### OUTRAM
Threads: green and blue/green
worked using the two needle and
thread method.

 ### NARROW BORDER
Two rows of back stitch worked in blue and
gold then a double row of wave stitch worked
in brick to form a diamond with an upright cross
in the centre worked in dusky rose.

In 1820 the effects of the Land Enclosures had reached
East Riding * Farmers had to find other means of livelihood
for their sons *John 1795-1858 a tailor left the farmstead and
moved to Holmfirth West Riding *m Mary Cartwright
elizabeth william henry george mary ann martha*

 ### ASPIRING TUSSOCK - FIVE ROWS
Threads: blue and blue/green using the two thread and
needle method.

 ### NARROW BORDERS
Two rows of back stitch one in gold and the other in antique lilac

 ### WANAKA MAZE
Stage 1 - 3 only with chain stitch worked between the
wrapped long tail chain. Brick and antique lilac.

 ### NARROW BORDERS
Three rows of stitching

Back stitch in antique lilac, wave stitch in gold and a second
row of back stitch in antique lilac.
Note how the row of wave stitch and lower band of back stitch
are started in a little from the edge of the material to allow
space for the Capital 'W' in William.

William 1821-1891 m Hannah Armitage john amman
martha fred harry willie emma mary ***Harry
1859-1928 m Mary Hannah Charlesworth arthur herbert
harold ***Harold 1891-1958 m Harriet Anne Lee dorothy
j ***Dorothy J 1923 m Brian Lodge david philip***

 ### TWO NARROW BORDERS
Roslyn: tussock grass blue/green, wave stitch blue and upright
cross brick.
Farm gate: blue

 ### DUNEDIN
Threads: blue and blue/green were worked together in
the two needle and thread method.

TWO NARROW BORDERS
Farm Gate worked in blue
Aspiring Tussock inverted with wave stitch in blue and tussock in
green/blue. Note how this border has breaks to fit around the
capitals 'O' and 'B'.

Our Braithwaites are of anglo saxon origin the name means
broadfield *** Research Dorothy J Lodge * Holmfirth

 ### OTAGO (entire pattern worked)
Threads: blue, blue/green, brick, rose, antique lilac and
green. The blue/green is used for the upper 'tussock'
and green for the lower 'tussock'. Rose is used for the straight
stitch in the centre of the pattern.
Note I have signed and dated my work in this section of
embroidery in antique lilac.

The edges are worked with five stitches the same length worked into one space. Alternative edging options can be found in Narrow Borders page 65.

To stitch your sampler

Work out the information you wish to include and start with the first row of your text following instructions for 'Placement of Text' pages 22 and 90. Bear in mind the additional information that can be conveyed by variations in text. My text was stitched using blue and brick with overcast squares stitched in blue and antique lilac.

To ensure that each generation was readily identified, I used both colour and size as a code. Each new generation begins with the name, and dates of birth and death, stitched in brick. The wives names are worked in blue and begun with a capital letter as is each husband. The children are listed in lower case lettering using the same blue thread with each child separated with an overcast square stitch worked in blue. Each generation is separated from the next with three overcast square stitches worked in antique lilac. Because lettering needs to be considered as a band of pattern, no attempt was made to keep the name and dates on the same line. This suited my purpose when the name of a new generation ended a line and the date began the next.

Note between each row of text I have worked a row of back stitch in blue and two rows of couching in gold on either side of the blue backstitch. Where a Capital reaches up into the next line or a tail of a letter comes down below the rest of the stitching there are breaks in the rows of stitching.

PATTERNS
Select the patterns you wish to use, the patterns I used are listed as a guide only:
Listed in order from the top. Otago variation; Braithwaite; Pembroke; Aspiring Tussock; Outram; Aspiring Tussock; Wanaka Maze (Stage 1 & 2 only) Dunedin; Otago along with a number of narrow borders.

See colour photograph page 75

Celebrating special events and personal achievements is very much part of the Dunedin and Otago culture. We are very proud of our Scottish Heritage and all that our founding fathers' achieved within a few years of their arrival in 1848. Dunedin was quickly established as the Edinburgh of the South Pacific with the first free school for Girls in the Southern Hemisphere and the Otago University. It was a Dunedin Presbyterian minister who first mooted the need for New Zealand women to have equal voting rights with men. Legislation was passed for this in 1893. The wealth that was generated by the Otago gold rush in the 1860's not only helped to build Dunedin, it also helped to establish other centres throughout New Zealand.

The Otago 150th year sampler was not graphed out, the only tacked guide line was down the left hand side for the text and the only planning was for the wording which was worked out on paper. Wessex Stitchery has such a wealth of Stitch Patterns and Narrow Borders, that it is easy to work in this way. To give added interest to this sampler I recorded in the sampler that we were in the middle of an El nino heat wave, when this piece was worked.

Mrs Foster's philosophy and system of working as evidenced from her writing, was

> *A Wessex needle......asks for no suggestion for pattern or design on paper or material; it can even produce good effects without any previous planning of the worker s thought and brain, for it has stitches of its own by the use of which patterns will, as it were, evolve themselves........*

Requirements

- Fabric: Antique white Glenshee 29 count linen 30 x 60 cm (12 x 24"). Allow generously for the length of the Sampler. Wessex Stitchery can be worked on different linen counts quite happily, see page 11 for recommended alternative linens.
- Threads as listed:

DMC stranded cottons: blue 931, blue/green 3816*, brick 356, rose 3722, gold 832, antique lilac 3041. The colours selected include blue and gold which are Otago's colours

One thread of stranded cotton was used throughout.

*Indicates DMC thread colour substituted for Anchor 876 used in the embroidery.

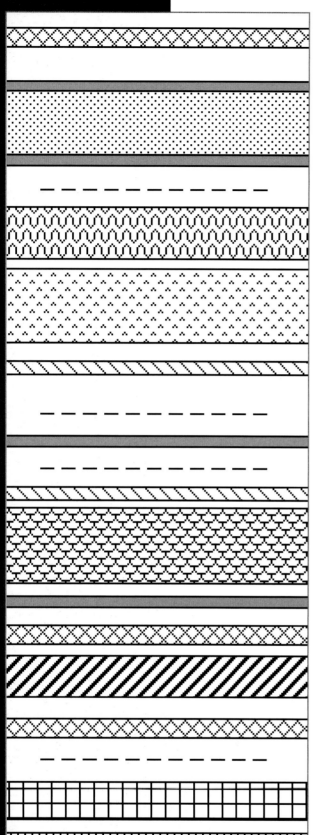

 **FARM GATE BORDER**

Worked using antique lilac

NARROW BORDER

Two rows of back stitch have been worked using blue and blue/green followed by two rows of wave stitch worked in blue to form a diamond then two more rows of back stitch worked in brick and blue.

 OUTRAM

Stitched using blue throughout.

NARROW BORDER

The back stitch and wave stitch border from above Outram has been inverted and repeated.

 *A little sampler to
commemorate the founding
150 years ago by the free
church of scotland the
majestic bountiful province
of Otago and the beautiful
city of Dunedin ♣♣♣
♣= four Dunedin pattern motifs

 IONA

The outer area of wave stitch has been worked in blue and rose, the central area has been worked using blue only

PEMBROKE (variation)

Blue and blue/green are the same value as each other and were worked together in the two needle and thread technique in this stitch pattern along with gold. A line of back stitch has been worked in blue at the top and lower edge of the stitch pattern.

ROSLYN

Two rows of wave stitch have been worked to form a diamond using blue with a central upright cross worked in brick. Two rows of back stitch in gold and blue are followed by aspiring tussock inverted and worked in antique lilac.

 *The john wickliffe 662 tons
arrived at port chalmers
with 81 passengers 23 march 1848

NARROW BORDER

Rows of wave stitch worked in blue with one row of wave stitch worked using rose. The lower row has been worked to form a diamond at the base of the border.

Philip laing 542 tons arrived with
246 passengers 15 april 1848

 ROSLYN BORDER

Aspiring tussock band has been worked in green and the two rows of wave stitch beneath it are worked in blue.

LINDISFARNE I

Threads: antique lilac, gold and blue/green with a line of back stitch worked in brick at the top edge of the pattern.

NARROW BORDER

Two rows of back stitch, the first worked in brick at the lower edge of the Lindisfarne pattern and the second in blue/green. Next two rows of wave stitch worked to form a diamond in antique lilac with a central upright cross worked in gold followed by two further rows of back stitch in blue/green and brick.

FARM GATE BORDER

Worked in blue

DUNEDIN

Blue and blue/green are the same value as each other and were worked together in the two needle and thread technique in this stitch pattern see page 19.

FARM GATE BORDER

Worked in blue

*This example of wessex
stitchery was worked during
the el nino heat wave of 1998

MORNINGTON

Note within this area of stitching I included my name and the date.

Threads: blue, rose, antique lilac and gold

FARM GATE BORDER

Worked in light antique lilac.

To Stitch Your Historical Record Sampler

Text

Work out the text you wish to include and start with the first row of your text following instructions for 'Placement of Text' pages 22 and 90. Work bands of lettering first leaving space for the bands of pattern. Bear in mind the additional information that can be conveyed by variations in text. In this instance the dates are highlighted by the use of different coloured thread.

Note: between each row of text I have worked one row of back stitch in blue with a line of couching in gold on either side. Where a capital reaches up into the next line or a tail of a letter comes down below the rest of the stitching there are breaks in the stitching.

Each word is separated by an overcast square in blue and I started most paragraphs with a single Outram motif in different colours.

Note: At the left hand side of the first block of text I have worked in gold, two vertical rows of wave stitch, that become diamonds. This narrow border was used to extend the first block of text. It has also allowed me to emphasize that block of text and to bring further gold into the embroidery. An attractive addition to the colour composition of the Sampler as well as representing one of the foundations of Otago's early settlement when gold mining was an important industry.

Patterns

Select the patterns you wish to choose, the patterns I used are listed as a guide only:
From the top down: Outram; Iona; Pembroke; Lindisfarne I; Dunedin , Mornington along with a number of narrow borders.

The edges are worked with five stitches the same length, worked into one space. Where Otago stitch pattern extended into the edge stitching, this stitching reverted to wave stitch.
As in all Wessex Stitchery experiment with colour combinations and enjoy the sheer fun of playing with needle and thread and the different combinations that you can create.

See colour photograph page 77

This Sampler was worked to commemorate the start of a new Millennium. I broke my rule of using just five to six colours because I wanted the Nigella stitch pattern border to include the colours of the Cheiranthus, a variegated perennial wallflower. The Cheiranthus flowers change colour as further buds open on the stem, it has a deliciously fragrant perfume and flowers through the winter giving wonderful colour and joy.

New Zealand is on the international date line and was the first country to see the dawn of the new millennium. Dunedin's Town Hall clock's midnight chimes 'rang in the dawn of the new era' around the world via Television New Zealand and the BBC. I included these details as I hope these comments will interest and intrigue future generations!

The Millennium sampler was worked in a different way. Because the message had to fit within a frame, I worked the top and a little of each side of the border pattern first, to establish the space. Then the text was fitted into the space given, with the final depth decided by the text and pattern.

Stitch Patterns:

Outside border Nigella page 45, internal bands Narrow Border Dunstan page 66.

Requirements and To Stitch

- Fabric: Glenshee, 29 count, ecru, for alternative linens see page 11.
- Threads as listed:

Nigella: DMC dusky rose 315, antique lilac 3041, gold 676, greens 469 and 581.

Optional extra: to give the look of the perennial wallflower the following DMC threads were selected randomly to work the little diagonal straight stitch that is between each 'Nigella flower'. Reds: 815, 305, 321, 3777*, Cerise 600, Rose pink 309 cyclamen 3687* pumpkin 922, gold 783.

This embroidery was stitched using DMC Perle 8 chosen for the glossy, 'frame' effect the thicker thread gave, alternatively use three threads of stranded cotton.

*indicates DMC thread colours substituted for Anchors colours 020 and 77.

Narrow Border Dunstan: DMC antique lilac 3041, greens 469 and 581.

One thread of stranded cotton was used in the three needle and thread blending method see page 19. The main fly stitch in this pattern is worked with the head and tail over two threads

The lettering was worked using one thread of stranded cotton and Alphabet II page 23. Dusky rose 315 was used for the main body of the text with dark red 815 used as a highlight and for the words I wished to emphasize. The text was underlined with couching worked using two threads of pale gold 676. There are breaks in the couching where the 'tail' of a letter comes below the main stitching.

NIGELLA

DUNSTAN

Beneath the rule of men entirely great, the pen
is mightier than the sword. **Bulwer-Lytton 1803-1873**

The **printing press** was the invention of the **second**
millennium A.D. that has brought the most benefit to
mankind. From **Johann Gutenberg's** invention in
1440 sprang an industry with extraordinary rapidity,
wherever the craving for literacy, **knowledge**
wisdom, truth, **freedom** and communication was
demanded.

My prayer for the **third millennium** is: Let
the pen be mightier than the sword so that the
lion will lay down with the lamb.

This little sampler was completed as **Dunedin's**
120 year old town hall clock's midnight chimes
rang in the dawn of the new millennium around
the world via television one **New Zealand**
and the BBC.

How to Hem and Mitre a Corner -

Preparation, refer to fig 1 - Tacking Guide

- Start and finish all tacked lines at the fabric edge. These tacked lines are your guide for a perfect mitred corner and are easily withdrawn once the hemstitching is complete. When tacking, do not finish off the ends, just leave ends of about 2 cm (1") trailing at the edge.

- Decide where the outer edge of the hem will be by either counting threads from the edge of the embroidery or measuring carefully and tack this - the dashed line - called the 'hem edge' carefully and accurately over four to six threads only. This is the most important tacking line.

- Decide the depth of your hem - traycloth 16 threads, needle case 8 threads. Count in 16 threads (traycloth) 8 threads (needlecase) from the 'hem edge' and work a second line of tacking - the solid line - called the 'stitch line'. The hem stitch will be worked along this line.

- Work a further line of tacking - the dotted line - called the 'turn under' 16 threads (traycloth) 8 threads (needlecase) beyond the 'hem edge'. The first fold for the hem is along this line.

- Trim the fabric beyond this outer line of tacking to a width less than the hem width - say 12 threads (traycloth) 5 threads (needlecase) and neaten in the usual manner see page 14.

- Each side of fabric now has three tacking lines.

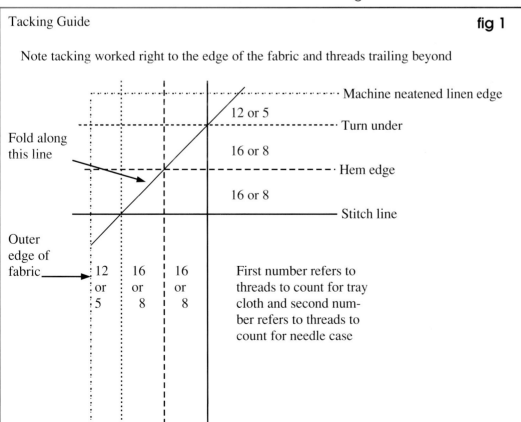

Tacking Guide   **fig 1**

Note tacking worked right to the edge of the fabric and threads trailing beyond

- Machine neatened linen edge
- 12 or 5
- Turn under
- Fold along this line
- 16 or 8
- Hem edge
- 16 or 8
- Stitch line
- Outer edge of fabric
- 12 or 5 | 16 or 8 | 16 or 8
- First number refers to threads to count for tray cloth and second number refers to threads to count for needle case

To Mitre the Corner

- Fold the corner down carefully where indicated. Carefully line up the tacking, pin to hold (fig 2). Fold a neighbouring corner down also, I find it helpful to prepare two corners at the one time.

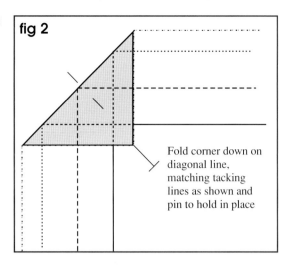

fig 2

Fold corner down on diagonal line, matching tacking lines as shown and pin to hold in place

- Fold along the 'turn under' tacked line (fig 3), finger press and position 'turn under' tacked edge on top of 'stitch line' tacking. Pin to hold in place.

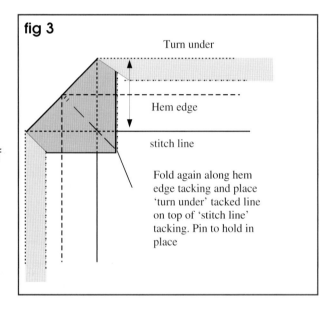

fig 3

Turn under

Hem edge

stitch line

Fold again along hem edge tacking and place 'turn under' tacked line on top of 'stitch line' tacking. Pin to hold in place

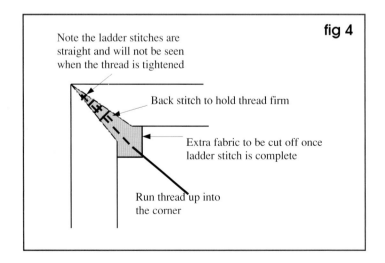

fig 4

Note the ladder stitches are straight and will not be seen when the thread is tightened

Back stitch to hold thread firm

Extra fabric to be cut off once ladder stitch is complete

Run thread up into the corner

- Join the mitre with ladder stitch see page 25. Use a fine tapestry needle (size 26) and matching thread, usually No 12 Perle cotton. Darn the thread into the corner of the mitre, hold in place with two backstitches above the hem stitch line and start ladder stitch at the outer edge of the mitre. Work down to the hemline (fig 4).

- Once the mitred corner has been joined lift it up and cut off the excess linen just above the hem line. It is easier to stitch each of the mitred corners first before working the hem stitching (fig 5).

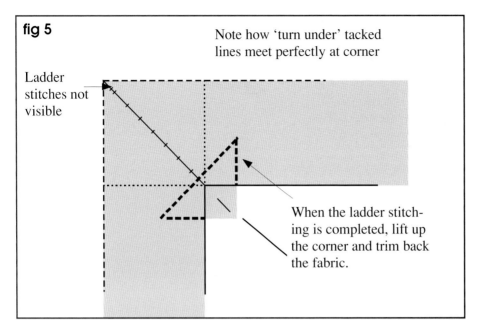

fig 5

Note how 'turn under' tacked lines meet perfectly at corner

Ladder stitches not visible

When the ladder stitching is completed, lift up the corner and trim back the fabric.

To hem stitch

- Pin the hem in place, check it is lying on the straight grain of the linen and stitch the hem in place by working hem stitch over the desired number of threads beginning at the mitred corner.

To Hem with a Matching Thread:

- Withdraw threads from the weave of the linen, short lengths only and keep twisting the thread as working.

FINGER CORDS

This style of finger cord was illustrated in a 1927 issue of 'The Embroideress' and is a very attractive and functional method of finishing many small items. It is a strong drawstring for the hussif and small bags and a useful way to cover the edges of pin cushions etc. Making your own cord has the advantage that it can be made using the thread used in the embroidery and it is easy to attach firmly within toggles, tassels and scissor tags as extra thread is left at both ends of the cord.

Instructions are given here for making the Hussif drawstring cord, as a general guide when making finger cord for other projects cut two lengths of thread four to five times longer than the finished length of cord required. If you have not made this cord before practice using Perle 3 or 5 thread or wool in two different colours. Because of the method of working extra thread is required for shorter lengths of cord.

Hussif Drawstring Cord

Two 45 cm (18") lengths of finger cord are required for the drawstring

1. Cut one six strand length 2.5m (2 3/4 yards) of DMC 501 stranded cotton. Divide it into two three strand lengths. This will give enough thread to attach the toggle and to work the detached buttonhole stitch that covers the ends.

2. Join the two lengths of three threads of stranded cotton with a simple knot, 10 cm (4") from the end. This 10cm (4") allows enough thread to attach the beginning of the cord to the toggle (fig 1).

3. Hold one length of thread firmly in your left hand.

4. Loop the other length of stranded cotton over the first finger of your right hand, twist the thread to close the loop (fig 2).

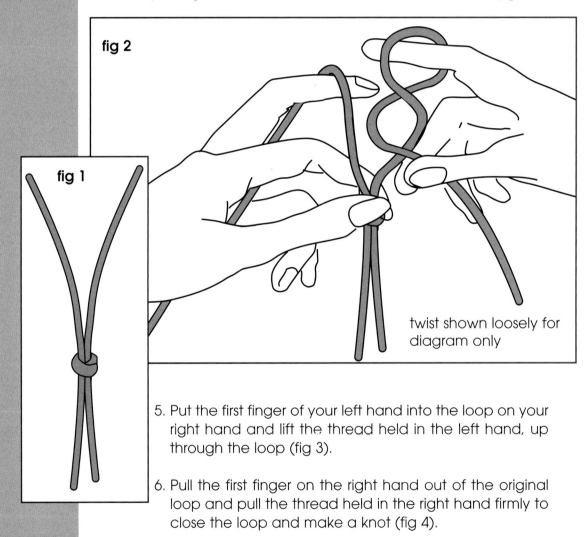

fig 2

fig 1

twist shown loosely for diagram only

5. Put the first finger of your left hand into the loop on your right hand and lift the thread held in the left hand, up through the loop (fig 3).

6. Pull the first finger on the right hand out of the original loop and pull the thread held in the right hand firmly to close the loop and make a knot (fig 4).

7. The loop just made, is now held over the first finger of the left hand.

8. Put the first finger of your right hand into the loop on your left hand and lift the thread held in the right hand up through the loop (fig 5). Now pull the first finger on the left hand out of the loop and pull the thread held in the left hand to close the loop and make a knot.

9. Repeat steps 5 to 8, changing from right hand to left, left hand to right. until the length of cord required has been made, leaving 45 - 50 cm (18- 20") of thread which is used to secure the cord into the toggle and work the detached buttonhole stitch to cover both ends of the roll.

10. To secure the completed cord, take the thread through the loop, pull to close.

HANDY HINT: Perle 8 would work well if the required colour was available. The advantage of hand made finger cord is that the same thread is used as was used in the embroidery ensuring a coordinated and superior finished appearance.

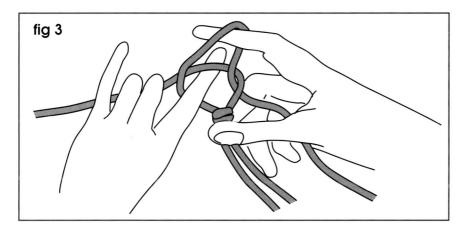

fig 3

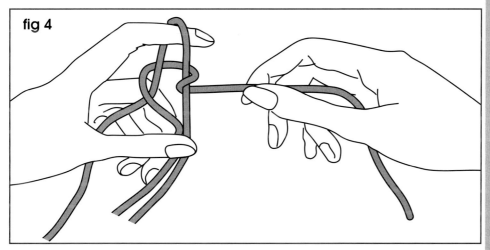

fig 4

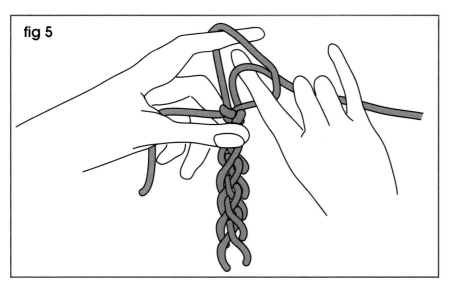

fig 5

TOGGLES

These attractive little toggles can be made to match any piece of embroidery you are working on.

1. Cut two pieces of linen 3.5 x 8cm (1 1/2 x 3 1/4").

2. Machine neaten all the raw edges.

3. Fold the long edges in to meet at the centre and press firmly. With matching thread tack the fold through the machine neatened edge near the centre, until 1 cm (1/2"), from the end (this will be turned under). As the tacking will remain in place once the toggle is complete, take a large stitch on the inside and a small one on the outside, leave the threaded needle attached to the fabric.

4. Roll the fabric very firmly to the last 1cm (1/2"), hold the roll together with a pin; turn under the 1cm and slip stitch in place using the tacking thread.

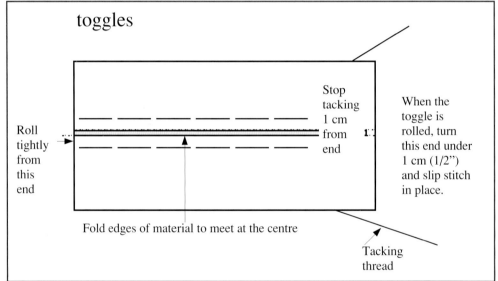

toggles

Stop tacking 1 cm from end

When the toggle is rolled, turn this end under 1 cm (1/2") and slip stitch in place.

Roll tightly from this end

Fold edges of material to meet at the centre

Tacking thread

To attach the Finger Cord to the Toggle:

1. First, thread the finger cord through the channel for the draw string at the top of the Hussif with a large tapestry needle. Take one cord in from each side. There will be two cord ends hanging from each side of the hussif.

2. Use a stiletto to make a hole at the centre of the side seam of a toggle, to carry the knot on the cord into it.

3. Thread one three strand 10cm end into a strong sharp needle. Take the needle into the hole at the side seam and right through to the opposite side of the roll, a thimble is very useful! On the outside of the toggle bring the thread back round to the side seam, put the needle back into the side seam bringing it out on the opposite side of the roll a second time. Bring the thread back round to the side seam - the thread lies over one half of the toggle only - take the thread to one end of the toggle to finish off securely.

Cord—use a stiletto to make hole big enough to take knot up into toggle

4. Repeat with the second 10 cm length but lie the thread on the other side of the toggle and finish the thread at the other end of the toggle. The needle enters and exits the toggle at the same place each time.

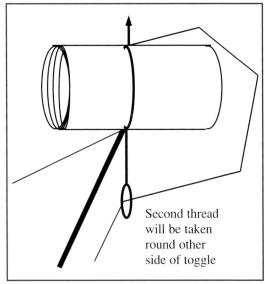

Second thread will be taken round other side of toggle

5. With your stiletto in the same position as before enlarge the hole to take the knot from the other end of the cord. Thread both lengths of thread into a sharp needle, take the long thread through the centre as before. Unthread the needle and thread three threads into a tapestry needle and bring the needle back round to the starting position, slide it down the seam line just under the fabric to come out three or four threads from the edge of the roll, ready to start the detached buttonhole stitching.

6. Work the first row of buttonhole stitch between every thread and over two fabric threads, from then on work detached buttonhole stitch. Start at the slip stitch seam, it is a guide to when a row is complete. Once the detached buttonhole has reached the end of the roll, decrease by missing every fifth stitch to nearly cover the roll end.

7. To complete, work a back stitch spiders web over the end using a coloured thread from your embroidery. Do this for each end of both toggles.

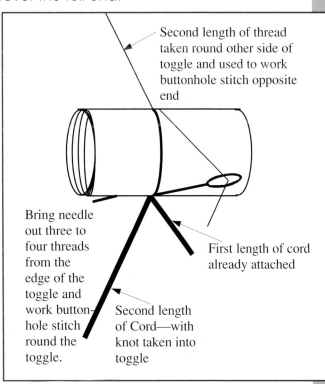

Second length of thread taken round other side of toggle and used to work buttonhole stitch opposite end

Bring needle out three to four threads from the edge of the toggle and work button-hole stitch round the toggle.

Second length of Cord—with knot taken into toggle

First length of cord already attached

FINISHING
Mounting, Framing & Care.

On completion of your embroidery it may need a little attention to look its best. Fine embroidery, for example the Braithwaite and Otago Samplers, may be placed face down onto a clean cloth and pressed on the wrong side to ensure it looks its best.

If a little puckering has occurred, or thick threads have created a little 'bulk', do not iron a pattern such as Wanaka Maze as it would destroy the textural quality of the embroidery, rather 'stretch' the embroidery in a manner similar to that used in crewel embroidery. This method is suitable for both small and larger pieces, textured or not.

• Be absolutely certain that the threads and fabric used are colour fast.

• Cover a soft timber (pinex or cork) board with kitchen foil and mark the actual size the piece should be by pinning tape onto the prepared board. (The foil protects your fabric from any possible staining from wet timber.)

• Prior to stretching, dampen with a water spray or wash the embroidery using a detergent without bleaches, perfumes, or additives then roll in a towel to absorb most of the moisture.

• Starting in the middle on each side, stretch and pin the embroidery out to the actual size marked with tape. Place the pins close to each other at 1 to 2 cm intervals along each side.

• Leave in an airy place to dry.
The work will not need to be ironed after being stretched in this manner.

HANDY HINT: any piece worked with perle cotton or tapestry wool should be stretched, not ironed.

When taking work into be framed ensure that acid free board will be used and glue will not hold your embroidery in place. Some framers will cut the board to size, for you to stretch and lace the work yourself.

To stretch and lace embroideries:

• ensure the fabric is kept straight to the grain
• use a good strong thread, i.e. No. 20 Mercerised crochet cotton
• start at the centre of each side and work out to each end, pulling the fabric taut and straight over the board.

An alternative to framing is to hem stitch the edge and make a channel or work button hole loops into the top hemline before threading a brass Bell Pull hanger or wooden or bamboo skewer through.

NAME & DATE YOUR WORK

It is important to work your name and date on all embroidery projects. Just initials are not good enough for major pieces because as time goes by they are not as likely to identify the worker. For most of us, it is the work that we leave behind that future generations will know us by. Other than Mrs Margaret Foster's embroidery, very little else is recorded of her long useful life.

TO EMBROIDER YOUR NAME ON CLOSELY WOVEN FABRIC:

• The counted thread method, tack a small piece of evenweave linen onto the hussif or needle case lining and work over it. Once completed, withdraw the linen threads

• Another method is to open and empty a tea bag, sign or print your name and date on this fine material; pin or tack it onto the lining; embroider over the printed line; (stem stitch worked over a signature is easily read) tear away once complete. Tea bag fabric is much less brittle than tissue paper.

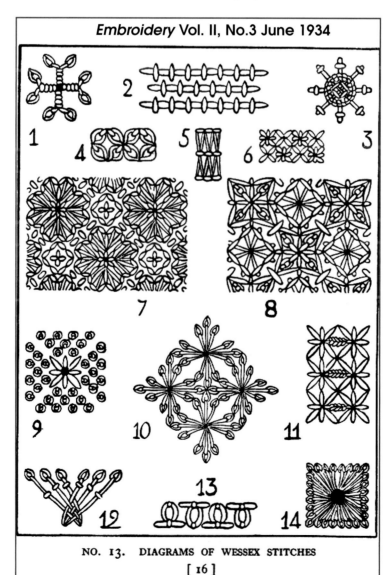

Embroidery Vol. II, No.3 June 1934

NO. 13.   DIAGRAMS OF WESSEX STITCHES
[16]

1. **Wanaka Maze**
2. **Couching**
3. **Dunstan Trail**
4. **Mercury Energy**
5. **United**
6. **Noughts and Crosses**
7. **Lindisfarne I**
8. **Nigella**
9. **Mountain Beech**
10. **Margaret**
11. **Pineapple**
12. **Bendigo**
13. **Not included**
14. **Mrs Foster**

On the Art of the Needle as shown in Wessex Stitching

WE all know that the subject of the little needle's art is one that reaches far and wide into history. With reverence it ventures to approach the sanctuaries of religion. It makes delicate and intimate entrance into the life of regal courts and quiet homes; it impresses on all who study its secrets the knowledge, so good to be known, that the love of beauty should not, and cannot, be quenched; that it is part of our better natures; that it is innate in man.[1]

What a fascinating vista lies fair to our memories only by recalling that these have been the ways of the needle; but I must not dally in these pleasant ways, for to-day I must speak only of one form, and that a new one, of would-be artistic sewing, one which does not even presume to call itself embroidery, but only stitching or stitchery. "Wessex stitching", let me call it, for it has been designed and worked chiefly in the old province where English fingers once gained the whole world's highest praise of the needlework; where embroidery was encouraged by kings and by men of sanctity and genius.[2] Very humbly does Wessex stitching seek admission to the world of art—that world where the fortunate workman finds his life's labour to be not only his task but also his pleasure: a pleasure, certainly, in one way checked, for no artist ever fulfils his own ideal. Unsatisfied longing for such fulfilment is, perhaps, his share of the home-sickness which all souls in exile must suffer. But, even so, to enter the art world is a privilege and a delight: Needlecraft has, indeed, long since entered there and has been given more or less honourable places, it has even been given "tolerated" places which it hardly deserved, for needlework of any kind, even at its worst, denotes so much of patience, of delicate fingering, of quiet homeliness, that it is sometimes preserved and cherished though sinning against every rule of art in technique, in design and in colour. In such cases it probably suffers from mechanical influence and aniline dyes; but it is handwork after all, therefore more respect is its due than if it were the actual product of machinery.

[1] The æsthetic sense shows itself in the earliest human work and among the rudest people. (From Architecture, by Professor T. J. Jackson).

[2] Especially by St. Dunstan, by St. Aldhelm and King Edward the Elder who, though great as King, warrior and statesman, yet found time to love embroidery and gave much encouragement to its execution.

3

The rules of art are strict, but they *are* also natural. They are the rules of nature and were never broken until workmanship was perverted by machinery. Wessex stitching steps forward fenced about by these rules, while its method is such that it cannot, if it would, disobey them. It does not aspire to outshine, not always to equal, the beautiful old, or some of the modern needlework of which many countries are justly proud, but with modesty (perhaps also apology) it makes new claims of its own.

The chief of these claims is the giving of entire independence to the needle. A Wessex needle requires no assistance from other implements any more than does the brush or pencil of the painter; it asks for no suggestion for pattern or design on paper or on material; it can even produce good effects without any previous planning of the worker's thought and brain, for it has stitches of its own by the use of which patterns will, as it were, evolve themselves, not requiring that whoever holds the needle should have natural power of design.

And here let me say a few words concerning all stitches. Of these the Wessex worker must certainly have good knowledge; it is a knowledge greatly neglected and by neglect of it many are deprived of a pleasure capable of adding a most pleasant fragrance to life. "The untrained eye cannot see what stares it in the face", nor the untrained ear enjoy all the sweetness of music. How very few eyes are trained to enjoy the beauty of needlework or to note its defects!

Castiglione would have his courtier "acquire knowledge of painting which at all events would enable him to appreciate the art of others".[1] To appreciate the art of embroidery all should acquire knowledge of what has been called "the witchery of stitchery", and stitches have indeed what I almost venture to call a sort of *Angel-witchery*, so simply and with such ease do they form designs fit for decoration. It may be said that each stitch is to embroidery what each note is to music, and the comparison may be followed on. Take the stitch as a note, the combining of stitches as a chord, and these (sometimes merely by repetition) flow into the pattern which forms the melody. Should not every house possess at least one sampler? A real *sampler*, an *example*; These for the use of all persons, not only for would-be embroiderers, but also for all who would "acquire a knowledge to enable them to appreciate the work of others", and thus add a joy to their own lives. There should,

[1] Il Cortigiano, by Castiglione.

of course, be other samplers for embroiderers, giving small specimens of patterns which the stitches have accomplished and which the worker may wish to preserve. It is good also (especially for children) to learn a pattern by heart as you would learn a song. In some cases a Wessex stitch has only to be learnt and then by repeating it (and given thread, needle and linen l) designs can be carried out as easily as one would fill a vase from a heap of gathered flowers.[1]

All the Wessex stitches and many of the designs they have created can be discovered—should anyone care to make the discovery—by study of the work in this exhibition. Of other stitches, also used by Wessex needles, full teaching is given in books on needlework. I will not encroach on their descriptions though I venture to advise the study of them. The voice of Embroidery whispers that, though perhaps held to be the humblest of arts, it is yet an art and, as such, pleads that no library should be without a volume of its history—ancient, mediæval and modern.

Another Wessex claim is that of requiring no previously pencil-drawn patterns. Thus the danger is avoided of deviating from the lines indicated. This danger is apt to be increased in a succession of copies until there ensues a result, as in the whispered secrets of the game called Russian Scandal, where, little by little, the original secret disappears. Probably in the case of an artist's design such deviation will spoil the beauty of proportion, perhaps the most essential beauty of any design and the one most easily lost.

And what of Wessex setting of its stitches? It is simple enough, for it is guided only by the threads of the work's foundation. I have heard that there is nothing new in this method though, until now, it had been very, very long since it was followed. In a lecture given at Granada a few years ago these facts were clearly pointed out. "In old embroideries", said the speaker, "the design was made not by drawing but by counting the threads. It is useless to try to reproduce old work by drawing the design. The only way is to count the number and direction of the stitches".[2] Wessex stitching had been started and, at intervals, worked for many years before this speech was made and I do not know to what old work it referred; I quote it lest I should seem to claim novelty for what seems to be very ancient.

[1] There are several old patterns of historical interest which should never be forgotten. The lily of Austria and succeeding nations, the lions of Egypt, the key and the honeysuckle of Greece, the strawberry, the acorn and another honeysuckle of England; all these and other can be reproduced Wessex-wise.

[2] From Speech by Manuel de Falla, 1922.

But this old work sounds somewhat difficult, the counting of its stitches rather tedious. Wessex work follows the threads of its foundation, but it asks, practically, for no counting of its stitches and gives no trouble whatever about the direction of its threads.

There exists, of course, no need of pencil in preparation of what is called "drawn work"; often very charming but following quite a different line of country from any other species of embroidery. It is in fact more of the use and nature of lace. There is none of it in this Exhibition. There is nothing shown here (save only in the separate section called "Wessex Exceptions") which is not entirely simple and original "Wessex stitching". There are here about 200 specimens of this new—shall I say "intruder"?—into the region of decorative sewing. All are worked by the same hand and no two pieces are alike. There exist more of such specimens, all different from each other and from those exhibited. These facts I mention to show how easily the stitches lend themselves to variety.

All the work is given the same generic title but it has different patterns to which, for convenience, specific names have been allotted. These names have been borrowed sometimes from places of particular interest in England—Croyland, for instance, and Beverley, both so famous for old stories, beautiful and true—sometimes from those ladies of the earliest England whom we know to have been lovers of their needles. St. Milburga is one of these. Her lovely life is forgotten in most parts of her country, but westward in England, among the Shropshire hills, the poor folk still keep her in remembrance.[1]

Most of these pattern names are explained on the work, in the lettering which Wessex needles have adopted. Many specimens are intended for *panels*, to be framed, others as *samplers* showing new stitches and patterns, also for framing. (*Pray note the difference between panels and samplers.*) There are, besides, bags for work or handkerchief and some very small specimens worked as needlebooks, tiny work-table pockets, lavender and cedar cases—lavender which gives its best to England; cedar so healthily fragrant, so gifted with the mystery of having been used to sweeten the Waters of Purification. But all these trifles have been worked more as specimens of the *stitching* and to teach its designs, than for their other uses. The design of each one, be it worthy or unworthy of notice,

[1] *St. Milburga was an English princess in the seventh century; she became Abbess of Wenlock and was greatly beloved and venerated there. The church at Buckbury in Shropshire is dedicated to her memory. Her Convent was destroyed by the Danes but the walls now standing in ruins at Wenlock were built on the same site.*

6

Is at least quite unique. There is not anywhere another like it.

But I am writing only to introduce a catalogue and this I think I have done. Perhaps too lengthily.

I present this Catalogue. Let it now speak for itself.

M.M.F.

7

FURTHER READING:

Wessex Stitchery:

Embroidery, Volume 11, Number 3, June 1934
Embroidery, Volume 23, Number 1, Spring 1972
The Embroideress, Volume 7, pages 1197 - 1199 (circa 1922-39)
Clabburn, Pamela, *The Needleworkers Dictionary*, Macmillan, 1976
Swift, Gay, *The Batsford Encyclopaedia of Embroidery Techniques*, Batsford, 1984
The Embroiderers' Guild, *Embroidery Studio*, David & Charles, 1993
The Embroiderers' Guild, *Making Samplers*, David & Charles, RD Press, 1993

Pattern Making & Colour:

Backhouse, Janet, *The Lindisfarne Gospels*, Phaidon Press Limited, 1981
Beaney, Jan and Littlejohn, Jean, *Stitch Magic*, Batsford, 1998
Dobie, Jeanne, *Making Colour Sing*, Watson-Guptill Publications, 1986
Field, Robert, *Geometric Patterns from Churches and Cathedrals*, Tarquin Publications, 1996
Langford, Pat, *Embroidery Ideas from Blackwork*, Kangaroo Press, 1999
Messent, Jan, *Designing with Motifs and Borders*, reprint Madeira Threads (UK) Ltd, 1998
Messent, Jan, *Designing with Pattern*, reprint Madeira Threads (UK) Ltd, 1998
Neich, Roger and Pendergrast, Mick, *Pacific Tapa*, David Bateman, 1997
Pendergast, Mick, *Te Aho Tapu The Sacred Thread*, Traditional Maori Weaving, Reed, 1987

Important influences:

Thomson, Jane, (ed), *Southern People*, Miss Helen M. Moran, Longacre Press in association with the Dunedin City Council, 1998.
Threads, Volume 34, Magazine of the Association of New Zealand Embroiderers' Guilds Inc. 1997
Threads, Volume 8, Magazine of the Association of New Zealand Embroiderers' Guilds Inc. 1984

Changes in Embroidery Education in Britain:

Howard, Constance, *Twentieth - Century Embroidery in Great Britain to 1939*, Batsford, 1981

History:

Crisp, Roger, *Wessex A Journey Through Two Thousand Years*, Wessex Books, 1999
King, Donald and Levey, Santina, *The Victoria & Albert Museum's Textile Collection Embroidery in Britain from 1200 to 1750*, V & A Publications, 1993
Staniland, Kay, *Embroiderers, Medieval Craftsmen*, British Museum Press, 1991
Encyclopaedia Britannica - Alfred the Great

Review *The Times* circa 2nd or 3rd March 1934, London

WESSEX STITCHERY

AN OLD LADY'S ACHIEVEMENT

An exhibition of Wessex stitchery was opened yesterday afternoon at the Medici Galleries, 7, Grafton Street, W., by Major Sir Nevile Wilkinson. It is expected that the Queen will visit the exhibition one day soon. It will remain open until March 15, each day from 9.30 a.m. to 6 p.m., and on Saturdays from 9.30 a.m. to 1 p.m. The work is that of Mrs. Forster, of Bath, a lady of over 90; it is all original in design and technique and is worked by the same hand.

Sir Nevile Wilkinson described Wessex stitchery as one of the most marvellous pieces of craftsmanship in the world, in which the little needle was used as a docile playfellow. Its creator sprang fully armed into the world of needlecraft, and her every mood passed over the patterns as wind over the cornfields. He knew her at Shafton, and she had done a great deal of work for Titania's Palace. England should be proud of craftsmanship of this calibre, and he urged those who loved needlework to follow in her footsteps—if they could.

A very large attendance crowded the gallery, and experts spent a busy time examining the wonderful stitches of the panels and samplers, of which there were about 300 pieces framed and unframed, and a number was sold during the afternoon. Lady Smith-Dorrien, principal of the Royal School of Needlework, was choosing specimens for her school.

This is Mrs. Forster's first exhibition, and 30 years' work is shown. Many pieces are dated, so that the changes in the art she has created can be noted. She has called her work "Wessex Stitchery," for the reason that Wessex was in Saxon times the centre of needlework and the art of illumination. She uses no designs, but writes and draws freely with her needle.

She says, in the introduction to her catalogue, that the chief claim of Wessex Stitchery is the giving of entire independence to the needle: it has stitches of its own by the use of which patterns will, as it were, evolve themselves, but requiring that whoever holds the needle should have natural power of design. The Wessex worker, however, must have a good knowledge of all stitches: each stitch is to embroidery what each note is to music, the combining of stitches a chord flowing into the pattern which forms the melody. The Wessex stitches and many of the designs they have created can be discovered, she says, by study of the work in the exhibition. The setting of the stitches is guided only by the thread of the work's foundation.

The exhibits express a robust patriotism and a deep sense of religion, shown in the many texts from Shakespeare, the Bible, St. Francis de Sales, and poets and saints of many centuries. Each text supplies the motif for the lovely stitchery, which varies in colour and movement with its theme. Inspiring words spoken by the Prince of Wales were the origin of one panel, a fine thought from Alexander Pope was the seed for another, Shakespeare's description of St. Margaret of Scotland gave rise to yet another, and among the fine thoughts and holy words are scattered little tags of garden lore, a delightful little flower panel coming to life from these lines:—

"These rules the gardener should not forget
To sow in the dry, to plant in the wet."

When Mrs. Forster reached the age of 90 it was thought that her eyes were failing her, and an oculist examined her. His report was that there was nothing wrong with her eyes, but that she was using glasses suited to an old lady and not to one as young in sight and mind as she was.